Gardner's Guide to

Internships in New Media

Garth Gardner, Ph.D.

Disclaimer

After publication of this manuscript, changes may occur in the internships and or internship programs at these companies. While reasonable efforts were taken to seek current information from appropriate offices at the companies, the responsibility for complying with all applicable requirements ultimately rests with the student or reader. This book does not attempt to profile the details of the company policies pertaining to internships. The applicant must contact each company for current policies regarding the application process for internships.

Nothing in this manuscript may be construed to promise or guarantee registration and acceptance in an internship program.

Editorial inquiries concerning this book should be addressed to the editor at GGC, Inc, MB# 3745, 4450 Rivanna Lane, Fairfax VA 22030-4441.

Gardner, Garth

Gardner's Guide to Internships in New Media: Computer Graphics, Animation & Multimedia/ by Garth Gardner.

p.   cm.

Includes bibliographical references and index.

ISBN 0-9661075-3-5 (pbk)

1. Internship guide—United States. I. Title.
2. New Media Internships—Art, animation, computer graphics, etc.
3. Multimedia Careers—Computer graphics careers, etc.
4. Computer Graphics Industry—Directory, guide, etc.
5. Internship and Programs—Hand book, reference, etc.

LC# 99 098079

About the Author

Dr. Garth Gardner is an associate professor and director of the multimedia minor at George Mason University's New Century College. A fine artist, Gardner's images are exhibited internationally. He has written several articles for national and international publications, and is the author of *Gardner's Guide to Computer Graphics, Animation and Multimedia Schools 2000*.

Acknowledgments

The author thanks the many people who have helped to produce this project: Editor Bonney Ford. Graphic Designer Nic Banks. Research Assistants Danielle Albanesse, Andrew Johnston, and Kim Alexander. Editorial assistant Terry Crump. Contributing writers Jenny Arata and Danielle Albanesse. I thank the associates of GGC, Inc., and gogardner.com for their invaluable support, and devotion in building this successful corporation.

Edited by Bonney Ford

Cover design and layout by Nic Banks

For students everywhere and especially for my students at

New Century College,

George Mason University

Contents

Introduction

Perhaps one of the most important decisions one must make in their academic career is finding the right major, a major area of emphasis, a major that best fits your personality and one that prepares you to attain your goals in a changing work-force. Though most academic programs in multimedia have some kind of internship course in the curriculum, others still rely on the student to do this work as an extra curriculum activity. Regardless of your school's policy regarding internships, note that an internship is a very important experiential learning opportunity. Internships serve as a means to bridge the gap between academia and the professional world. They serve as the means to continue where your school may have fallen short or to solidify the theories you have learned. Internships give you the opportunity to "test drive" a career. They can give you the opportunity to earn extra academic credit. They allow you to see from the inside, to test whether a particular career is right for you. Beyond being real world experience, it also provides students with a venue for networking with professionals in their areas of emphasis. In the case of the multimedia student then an internship opportunity can also be an opportunity to work on professional projects that may lead to an improved demonstration reel and portfolio. Finally an internship often offers students a chance to work on a production team where all members are well established in their areas of specialization. Internships add practical experience to your résumé.

This book is designed to equip students with the necessary knowledge for finding an internship in the field of new media, computer graphics, animation, web page design, television production, graphic design and many other areas. The primary purpose of this book is to guide students in the area of multimedia to various internship opportunities available to them. There are various other steps a student must take beyond the initial search for internship, some of which may be: submitting a résumé and portfolio, arranging for a phone interview, interview in person. Taking these steps into consideration, this book will offer basic guidelines to assist students through these subsequent procedures.

This is truly a great field to be a part of; there is no other field like it that offers such excellent opportunities for artists and scientists. With the Internet market on a constant incline, career opportunities for practitioners in this field are endless. Today trained web artists and programmers are commanding salaries that rival that of doctors and lawyers, and trained graphic designers and animators are working more efficiently with the aid of the computer.

Where To Start

Start by making an appointment to speak with a career counselor at your school to discuss your career goals and objectives. You must first figure out what area of new media most intrigues you. Explore the options on paper. When you have decided on an area or combination of areas, begin the search. Look first at the major companies that specialize in your area of interest. Select at least 20 primary companies that you would like to target. Visit the web sites of these companies to get a general understanding of what they do, available internships, deadline information and requirements for applying for an internship. In most cases they simply need to have a cover letter and résumé. E-mail the director or coordinator of the internship program and get a general feel for the ratios of acceptance. Do not be intimidated by the large pool of applicants to the internship program. Do make sure that you have fulfilled the requirements necessary for an internship at the company and that you are working within the deadline. Be practical about your decision. Remember that some internships require an in-person interview. Be realistic and plan ahead. It is not unusual for students to already have dozens of leads for a summer internship by mid-fall of the previous year.

When To Apply For An Internship

Although students who are seniors in high school to college seniors are eligible to apply for internships at a new media company, the most commonly acceptable group are students at the college junior and senior level. Interns must be returning to college at the end of the internship program. This is a requirement at most companies. Students may apply for an internship as early as a year in advance. In fact the most common deadline for internships is mid-November of the preceding year for summer internships. Other internships are rolling and accept for an average period of three months all year round. Others are very loose and accept on an as-needed basis, without any deadlines. Therefore you must start in your freshman year to find an internship for your sophomore year. The is advisable for students in the animation, web design and other areas that are extremely competitive. This way if you are not successful in finding an internship in your sophomore year, you can try for your junior year.

G.P.A. Requirements

Although the acceptable grade point average (G.P.A.) for internships can vary, I have yet to come across an internship program that accepts students below a 2.5 G.P.A., and these are rare. The average G.P.A. for most internship programs is 3.0 and above, 3.5 for the most competitive internship programs at popular companies. Other companies may look at the G.P.A. from the major subjects only, and may not consider such subjects as Mathematics, and the Sciences to be relevant. Though most are looking at the package deal, i.e. the personality, educational rank, and interest in the subject area, it often the G.P.A. that is considered the first criteria for evaluating prospective interns.

Payment Issues

Yes it is a fact that most companies do not pay interns for their time, and also they do not charge interns either. The internship program is a learning experience for the students and a primarily teaching one for the company. Every intern hired must be trained and that is a costly undertaking for the company. According to a visual effects supervisor at a major California company "we had an intern that would walk in front of the set at times when we were shooting and we would have to re-shoot the entire scene." It is a fact that inexperienced individuals can be costly to a company. But not all are non-paid internships; some companies provide interns with a travel allowance for travels to and from work. Others pay a monthly stipend and some pay a minimum wage. Keep your eyes on the larger picture; you are not there to get a salary; you are there primarily for the experience and to make meaningful connections, and most importantly to learn more about the field that excites you. If you are one to say "no pay no way" you will be looking at a limited pool of possibilities.

Foreign Students

Foreign students may obtain an internship in the US. but must comply with the regulations of the Immigration and Naturalization Services (INS). Often prospective employers welcome these students but do not welcome the documents that are necessary for them to gain employment in the US. Usually an issued letter of acceptance from the employer is the key document for the foreign student to file through their school for an off-campus internship. In most cases if the internship is a part of the academic requirement for obtaining a degree at the school, the permission is granted. In this case the student is also free to accept monetary compensation if applicable. Foreign students' seeking an internship must first see the foreign students advisor at their school for detailed advice on these and other procedures relating to employment in the US.

Résumés And Cover Letters

Before you are called for your first interview, you must first attract your employer with your résumé and cover letter. Whether you are applying for an entry level position or Vice-President, your résumé and cover letter should stand out above the rest. Résumés are an outline, briefly yet concisely describing your educational history, work experience and computer skills. Be brief and to the point, highlight things in bold, and use bullets when necessary. Try to avoid getting personal, such as including hobbies. Focus on your employment strengths and skills. With modern technology, résumés can journey to the attention of a potential employer with the click of a mouse. Résumés can be sent through e-mail, snail mail, fax, and posted on the Internet. If you have difficulty writing your own résumé, there are services available for résumé writing.

New Media Résumé Recommendations

Perhaps you are all prepared for the new century and you have put together a résumé that has the look and feel of the year 2000 and beyond, one that is on-line, designed for interaction, and accessible through your web site. Presenting such résumé may not be such a good idea, especially when you are dealing with an established media company which has just embarked on the area of new media and may be apprehensive or simply not equipped to view disk or interactive versions of your résumé. To them, anything beyond print sends off a red light. As a prospective intern, stick to the traditional one page printed résumé. If you wish, create an interactive résumé as a secondary option. Most companies today receive at least 10 résumés for every one position available. Most do not accept attached e-mail résumés. Your prior education and employment history are the prime factors used by prospective employers for selection.

Here are some tips on preparing for and handling a prospective employer if you have a résumé that shows a variety of experiences:

Put your new media experience at the top. Throw out that idea that your résumé needs to be in chronological order. Don't make them search for your new media experience when that's what they're most interested in. This goes for your portfolio as well. Make sure everything in your portfolio is prominently displayed. Only include new media projects and drawings if they are incredible, or help to explain some aspect of the project. Such drawings may be incorporated in a story board for a future or present project.

Delete the jobs that do not relate to your goals today. It is always tempting to include the waitstaff job that you did at the fast food restaurant, but before you do so, think twice. If you have not had any experience in the field of new media and you are just breaking ground, that job as a waiter should stay. It will work for you. It shows the prospective employer that you have worked on a professional team and with a great reference, it can help to establish that you work well with others. Remember that the new media environment is very much team-oriented. On the other hand, if you have experience working on a multimedia project, and you are simply looking to get an internship to get in the door of a major company, delete the waiter position. In this case the information will help to establish that you are focused and goal-oriented. If you are in a position where you have interned in different areas of media, for instance, and you have got a super-résumé and cannot decide whether or not you should cut out your awards, toss your TV news experience first. Most newspaper employers do not think much of this medium, and you would not have any clips from it anyway. Some prospective employers might even look down on you for it, and it is not worth the risk. People in television want to see television experience on your résumé and those in web design want to see web design experience and that is the bottom line.

Praise your medium. Though you are only looking for an internship it is not to early too present yourself with a certain degree of confidence and loyalty to the field you have chosen to study. You may not be totally convinced which area of new media you would like to pursue; however, in the world of big business and large corporation, division of the various areas of new media has led to specialization. If your intention is to eventually work at a large multimedia corporation, you may want to start today to develop a commitment for an area of new media. Prospective employers want to know that as an intern you will continue to develop in an area of new media. Know the facts and speak knowledgeably about an area of new media that you enjoy. Discuss some advantages of this area on traditional media.

Five Basic Résumé Designs

Sample Résumé 1

Chris Jones

123 Main Street Anytown USA 55555 · (555) 555 5555
E-mail: chris@anywhere.com · URL: http://www.anything.com

software knowledge

Flash (2 yrs), Lightwave (2 yrs), Composer (6 mo's), Adobe Illustrator
(1yr), Adobe Photoshop (learning), Windows NT, Mac OS

experience

Yapping Pup Productions
June 1998 - Feb. 1999
Technical director
Worked on corporate logos including "WCAT" in Baton Rouge, and
"Here's Your Mattress" for The Mattress Warehouse in Murfreesboro.

Gogardner.com
July 1997 - Dec. 1998
Animation assistant
Assisted with web-based animation for corporate websites.

education

George Mason University, Any City
1998-present

State College or University, Any City
attended 1992-1994

relevant coursework

1 semester CAD, 2 semesters shell scripting in C++, 2 years Light
wave training. 8 semesters traditional painting, 8 semesters computer
animation, 6 semesters traditional cell animation.

other

I own a PC and love coming up with my own animation. I am
currently working on a 30-minute 3D animation about snowboarding
which I have scripted and storyboarded.

chris jones

123 Main Street Anytown USA 55555 · (555) 555 5555
E-mail: chris@anywhere.com · URL: http://www.anything.com

software knowledge	Flash (2 yrs), Lightwave (2 yrs), Composer (6 mo's), Adobe Illustrator (1yr), Adobe Photoshop (learning), Windows NT, Mac OS
experience	Yapping Pup Productions June 1998 - Feb. 1999 Technical director Worked on corporate logos including "WCAT" in Baton Rouge, and "Here's Your Mattress" for The Mattress Warehouse in Murfreesboro. Gogardner.com July 1997 - Dec. 1998 Animation assistant Assisted with web-based animation for corporate websites.
education	George Mason University, Any City 1998-present State College or University, Any City attended 1992-1994
relevant coursework	1 semester CAD, 2 semesters shell scripting in C++, 2 years Light wave training. 8 semesters traditional painting, 8 semesters computer animation, 6 semesters traditional cell animation
other	I own a PC and love coming up with my own animation. I am currently working on a 30-minute 3D animation about snowboarding which I have scripted and storyboarded.

Sample Résumé 3

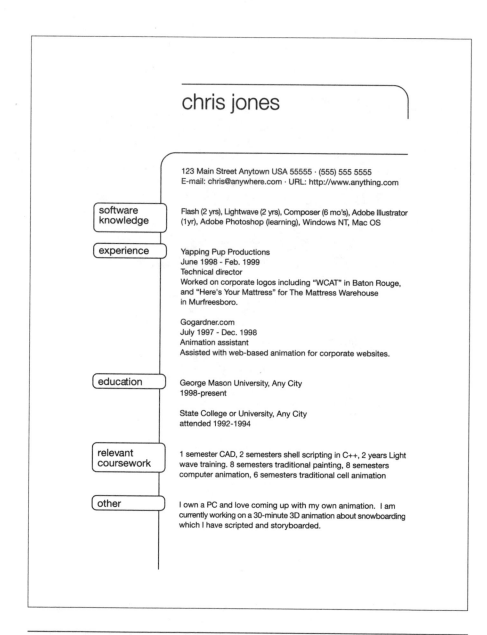

chris jones

123 Main Street Anytown USA 55555 · (555) 555 5555
E-mail: chris@anywhere.com · URL: http://www.anything.com

software knowledge

Flash (2 yrs), Lightwave (2 yrs), Composer (6 mo's), Adobe Illustrator (1yr), Adobe Photoshop (learning), Windows NT, Mac OS

experience

Yapping Pup Productions
June 1998 - Feb. 1999
Technical director
Worked on corporate logos including "WCAT" in Baton Rouge, and "Here's Your Mattress" for The Mattress Warehouse in Murfreesboro.

Gogardner.com
July 1997 - Dec. 1998
Animation assistant
Assisted with web-based animation for corporate websites.

education

George Mason University, Any City
1998-present

State College or University, Any City
attended 1992-1994

relevant coursework

1 semester CAD, 2 semesters shell scripting in C++, 2 years Light wave training. 8 semesters traditional painting, 8 semesters computer animation, 6 semesters traditional cell animation

other

I own a PC and love coming up with my own animation. I am currently working on a 30-minute 3D animation about snowboarding which I have scripted and storyboarded.

Chris Jones

123 Main Street Anytown USA 55555 · (555) 555 5555
E-mail: chris@anywhere.com · URL: http://www.anything.com

software knowledge

Flash (2 yrs), Lightwave (2 yrs), Composer (6 mo's), Adobe
Illustrator (1yr), Adobe Photoshop (learning), Windows NT,
Mac OS

experience

Yapping Pup Productions
June 1998 - Feb. 1999
Technical director
Worked on corporate logos including "WCAT" in Baton Rouge,
and "Here's Your Mattress" for The Mattress Warehouse
in Murfreesboro.

Gogardner.com
July 1997 - Dec. 1998
Animation assistant
Assisted with web-based animation for corporate websites.

education

George Mason University, Any City
1998-present

State College or University, Any City
attended 1992-1994

relevant coursework

1 semester CAD, 2 semesters shell scripting in C++, 2 years
Light wave training. 8 semesters traditional painting, 8 semesters
computer animation, 6 semesters traditional cell animation.

other

I own a PC and love coming up with my own animation. I am
currently working on a 30-minute 3D animation about
snowboarding which I have scripted and storyboarded.

Chris Jones

software knowledge
Flash (2 yrs), Lightwave (2 yrs), Composer (6 mo's), Adobe
Illustrator (1yr), Adobe Photoshop (learning), Windows NT,
Mac OS

experience
Yapping Pup Productions
June 1998 - Feb. 1999
Technical director
Worked on corporate logos including "WCAT" in Baton Rouge,
and "Here's Your Mattress" for The Mattress Warehouse
in Murfreesboro.

Gogardner.com
July 1997 - Dec. 1998
Animation assistant
Assisted with web-based animation for corporate websites.

education
George Mason University, Any City
1998-present

State College or University, Any City
attended 1992-1994

relevant coursework
1 semester CAD, 2 semesters shell scripting in C++, 2 years
Light wave training. 8 semesters traditional painting, 8
semesters computer animation, 6 semesters traditional cell
animation.

other
I own a PC and love coming up with my own animation.
I am currently working on a 30-minute 3D animation about
snowboarding which I have scripted and storyboarded.

123 Main Street
Anytown USA 55555
(555) 555 5555

E-mail: chris@anywhere.com
URL: http://www.anything.com

Web Résumé Sample

ANY PERSON
1111 Main Street
City, State 12345
Phone: 123-456-5555
Fax: 987-654-5555
E-mail: anyperson@address.com

SUMMARY OF QUALIFICATIONS
Animation student with extensive traditional animation experience. Expertise includes developing and implementing characters. Excellent storytelling and oral communication skills.
Applications: Maya; 3D Studio Max; Macintosh design software applications.
Program Languages: C, C++, UNIX and HTML coding.

KEY ACHIEVEMENTS
Teaching Assistant for Animation Course, Fairfax, VA 1999-present
George Mason University
Worked with the faculty and assisted with the evaluation of students' performance in the course. Reviewed papers and animation projects. Took daily attendance.

Assisted the students to achieve the course objectives. Lead individual sessions with students to review the technical aspects of the course. Taught animation software, and reviewed animation techniques. Assisted students with drawing tools on the computer. Organized group activities and field trips. Maintained relations with the students through office hours.
Director, Animated Film for MTV- 1998-1999
Independent Project.

Wrote and proposed film concept to MTV. Created animation storyboard and wrote script. Organized presentation and proposed budget for the film. Managed all functions of the animation production, organized staff, lead daily discussion with the animation team. Managed an animation budget of $30,000.

Worked with recruitment firm to select qualified staff members for the project. Reviewed portfolios/resumes and hired the management staff for the film.

EDUCATION
M.F.A. Computer Animation, 1998-expected in 2001
B.A. Multimedia, New Century College, George Mason University, 1998

Feel free to e-mail me any question: anyperson@address.com

Sample HTML Script For Creating Résumé On The Web

```
<HTML>
<HEAD>
<TITLE>Any person résumé</TITLE>
</HEAD>
<BODY BGCOLOR="#ffffff">
<TABLE WIDTH="450" BORDER="0" CELLSPACING="2" CELLPADDING="0">
<TR>
<TD WIDTH="100%"><P ALIGN=CENTER>RÉSUMÉ OF ANY PERSON</P>
<P>ANY PERSON<BR>
1111 Main Street<BR>
City, State 12345<BR>
Phone: 123-456-5555<BR>
Fax: 987-654-5555<BR>
E-mail: anyperson@address.com<BR>
<BR>
<B>SUMMARY OF QUALIFICATIONS </B><BR>
<BR>
Animation student with extensive traditional animation experience.  Expertise
includes developing and implementing characters. Excellent storytelling
and oral communication skills. </P>
<P> Applications: Maya; 3D Studio Max; Macintosh design software applications.</P>
<P> Program Languages: C, C++, UNIX and HTML coding. <BR>
<HR ALIGN=LEFT></P>
<P><B>KEY ACHIEVEMENTS </B></P>
<P><B>Teaching Assistant for Animation Course</B>, Fairfax, VA 1999-present</P>
<P>George Mason University</P>
<P> Worked with the faculty and assisted with the evaluation of students' performance in
the course.  Reviewed papers and animation projects. Took daily attendance.</P>
<P> Assisted the students to achieve the course objectives. Lead individual
sessions with students to review the technical aspects of the course.  Taught
animation software, and reviewed animation techniques. Assisted students
with drawing tools on the computer. Organized group activities and field
trips.</P>
<P> Maintained relations with the students through office hours.<BR>
</P>
<P><B>Director, Animated Film for MTV</B>- 1998-1999 </P>
<P>Independent Project.</P>
<P> Wrote and proposed film concept to MTV. Created animation storyboard
and wrote script. Organized presentation and proposed budget for the film.</P>
<P> Managed all functions of the animation production, organized staff, lead daily
discussion with the animation team. Managed an animation budget
of $30,000. </P>
<P> Worked with recruitment firm to select qualified staff members for the project.
Reviewed portfolios/resumes and hired the management staff for the film.<BR>
<HR ALIGN=LEFT></P>
<P><B>EDUCATION </B></P>
<P>M.F.A. Computer Animation, 1998-expected in 2001</P>
<P>B.A. Multimedia, New Century College, George Mason University, 1998 </P>
<P><HR ALIGN=LEFT></P>
<P>Feel free to e-mail me any question: <A
HREF="mailto:%22anyperson@address.com">anyperson@address.com</A></P>
<P><BR>
</TD></TR>
</TABLE>
</BODY>
</HTML>
```

Cover Letter

Cover letters can help you express your interest in the employer, your qualifications, requirements, and your availability for an interview. The cover letter allows you to include information not stated in the résumé. Cover letters are sometimes overlooked, but it is still essential to include one with your résumé. The cover letter should be written with conciseness and clarity. Remember you are a professional, and your cover letter represents you. Résumés and cover letters are your first step in the door, followed by the interview. However, before you can get to the interview, you must be able to sell yourself in writing.

A Winning Cover Letter

The fact that most internships are highly competitive means that the intern applicant must pay closer attention to the cover letter. Put yourself in the employer's position for a minute, with over 10-100 applicants competing for every available internship position, each with similar backgrounds. How would you make the choice; what would be the deciding factors? Your cover letter is your first written contact with the company, and it may well be your only chance to convince them that, of the hundreds of applicants that they may have reviewed recently, you are a strong contender for the position. In a pool of résumés that sounds and looks similar, a well-constructed cover letter can give you the edge. The following template concepts are based on approaches recommended by Joe Grimm, recruiting and development editor of the Detroit Free Press.

Be original not bland

Though it may be tempting and more straight forward to go with the traditional bland cover letter, this will not help to get the attention of the employer. For example, come up with some creative ways of introducing yourself. Remember that you are applying for a creative position in a new media. Try to <u>avoid</u> opening your cover letter with one of the following phrases.

• I am applying for a summer photo internship with the Daily Tidings because I know I can do the job well.

• I currently am a senior majoring in journalism and minoring in psychology at Party Tech. In addition, I…

• My name is Slim Shady, and I am a sophomore in the process of completing a bachelor's degree in journalism at Ivy League University.

Do not get wordy

Get to the point quickly. Avoid these approaches:

• I am currently looking for a summer internship in the new media industry and would like to be considered for such a position at your newspaper. I am a junior in college pursuing a concentration in print-journalism and would very much appreciate a chance to apply what I have learned to a premiere new media company, such as yours.

• It has come to my attention through an advertisement at George Mason University that intern positions in feature animation are available at your studios.

• I am writing to express my interest in an internship at ILM over the coming summer.

• I would like to use this letter as an opportunity to introduce myself as a qualified candidate for the summer internship program at the Pixar Studios.

Tell a story

New media designers are often expected to produce convincing designs that tell a story about a product. Here is your opportunity to show the company that you can. If you take this approach, say — quickly — what the point of the story is.

• Each day, Barb Shook carried an armful of shirts into the dry cleaners, and picked up a few clean ones, neatly pressed and bagged in plastic. Working the counter to pay for my journalism studies, I was intrigued by the woman with all the shirts. Finally, I just had to ask …

• It's surprising how quickly you can wear out a pair of shoes on the streets of Chicago…

• When Jim Johnson appeared to chase his family out of the house and then set fire to it, the neighbors thought he was acting crazy again. It turns out, he was a hero.

• My parents told me that if I was going to go out of state to go to school, then I'd have to get there on my own. In a borrowed car that became my living quarters for the next four days, I did.

The experienced approach
Many internship candidates have only slight experience. If you have loads of experience to offer — especially if it's in commercial, multimedia production, let them know.

• In two summer internships, I have assisted in the design and planning of over 10 web sites for companies such as Ford and General Motors.

• As the Webmaster of my department, I am chiefly responsible for designing the department's web site.

• Few animators my age can say that they wrote all of the software used in the creation of an animation.

• I have endured horseflies, poison ivy, angry dogs and downpours to get a good quote or a telling detail for a story…

The direct approach
If you're proud of who you are and a what-you-see-is-what-you-get person, try the fresh and straightforward approach. What would you tell the employer, face to face, games aside, about why they should hire you? Avoid wordy. Be crisp, not bland.

• Please accept my application for a photo internship at the Detroit Free Press. I believe that my experience at school and in a prior internship, as well as my knowledge of the area make me a strong candidate for your newspaper.

• Hire me for a photography internship because I work tirelessly, find excellent photo opportunities everywhere and develop them well.

• My passion is to create animation…

The twist approach
Wake up the reader with a twist or a tease. Play contradiction, irony or the unexpected to maximum advantage. Remember that one of the key things employers want to find in a good cover letter is evidence that you can write.

• Like most student designers, I expected to start at the bottom as the "go for" at an interactive studio, planning getting coffee, answering phones. That's not what I got, though, when I showed up for the first day of work last summer…

• Sometimes, the stories I tell amaze me…

• It's been said that you're only as good as your last animation. Let me tell you what it was…

• I have to admit, I wasn't excited the first time I was asked to create a design for a user interface.

The confident approach
A narrow line to walk, be bold without being brash, assured without being arrogant. Only you can tell whether such an approach is natural to you.

• I am exactly the right person for your sports-writing internship!

• Are you looking for a highly motivated, team-centered, up-and-coming photographer who is hard working and creative? I am that person.

• There are few guarantees in life. I am one. Hire me, and you will not be disappointed.

• The person you have been looking for has applied.

Autobiographical approach

Can you tell a story about yourself that explains why you are an excellent prospective intern? Some people can begin their letters in these ways:

- My family always said I loved to tell stories.

- Perhaps it's my sense of order that led me to newspaper design.

- Since the age of 8, I have known that this was the right business for me.

- Maybe it was destiny, because it sure wasn't heredity.

- As a senior in high school, I swore I'd never leave my home and family. I did, though, kicking and screaming, and it was the best thing I ever did.

Interviewing

A woman walks into an interview wearing a pants suit with her résumé in hand. She carries herself with confidence. Taking a deep breath and with a firm handshake she says, "Hello Mr. Smith, I'm Jane Doe. Pleased to meet you." From the moment Jane walked through the door, the interview had begun. Interviewing is crucial to landing the perfect job, and it is more than showing up and filling out an application. Think of it as going on a first date, where you want to make a positive first impression. During an interview, hopeful applicants are put under the microscope, and evaluated in every way from appearance to skills. You are a product on display, wanting to become an asset to the company. Therefore, you must prepare yourself. In preparation for the interview, know your strengths and weaknesses because you will most likely be asked to analyze those characteristics. Think about what your response will be to questions like "What do you expect from your supervisor?" "Where do you see yourself in five years?" "Why do you think you would be a good fit for this organization?" Answer directly, try not to ramble or reveal negative information about yourself. Write down your answers if you have to, whatever helps to build your confidence for the interview. Get a friend to play-act an interview, so that you can practice. Mannerisms are equally important: relax, sit-up straight and do not slouch or fidget. If you have a tendency to fidget excessively, such as uncontrollable leg shaking or nail biting, try to control it because you might appear less relaxed and confident. Eye contact with the interviewer is considered a sign of confidence. Keep in mind that your employer will expect you to have questions of your own. Some questions you might want to ask: "Is there room for advancement?" "Does Company X have a tuition reimbursement program?" Do not hesitate to ask any other possible questions you might have, and of course, you should remain confident during every aspect of the interview, including when you take the floor. Dress in appropriate business attire, and carry yourself with class and confidence. As we enter the new millennium, employers will continue to require an interview for virtually every job opening. Hopeful candidates will prepare themselves for what can be the difference between employment and an on-going search in the classifieds. An interview can make or break your chances. Good luck!

Interview Questions

• Prepare questions to ask your interviewer. For example:

• What are some of the tasks and projects I will be involved in?

• What are your expectations of an intern who works for your organization?

• What is the dress code of your organization?

• Will I have the opportunity to meet regularly with my internship supervisor?

• What sort of training or orientation with I receive?

• How many hours per week will you want me to work?

• Will there be a salary, stipend or college credits for my work there?

• Will I receive reimbursement for my travel expenses?

• Will I be covered by workers' compensation if I am injured at my internship site?

• What is the duration of the internship?

Be prepared to answer the following questions in your interview, these are some commonly asked questions:

- Are you familiar with our company, services and products?

- Why do you want an internship at this company?

- What objectives do you hope to obtain through this internship?

- What are your career goals?

- What are your greatest strengths and biggest weaknesses?

- Beyond your class projects what meaningful projects have you been involved in? why was this meaningful?

- Beyond your academic program, have you worked on team projects? Talk about your experience.

- We have several candidates for this internship position, why should we choose you?

- Who is your least favorite manager? Why?

- How would you resolve conflicts between your academic schedule and surprise, rush jobs here?

Things To Take To The Interview

- Copy of your résumé and cover letter.

- Portfolio, sides, video, drawings etc.

- Copy of college transcripts, especially if it has changed since you submitted the internship application.

- Copy of completed application for internship.

- A positive attitude and enthusiasm for the field of New Media.

Interview Thank You Letter Sample

January 12, 2000

1212 Main Street
Fairfax, VA

Ms. Bonney Ford,
Marketing Director
GGC, Inc.
1212 John Doe Lane
Fairfax, VA

Dear Ms. Ford:

Thank you so much for taking the time from your busy schedule last Thursday to interview me for the internship position at GoGardner.com. After our meeting, I am convinced that your company is the best place for me to learn about e-commerce and web design, my long-term career goal.

As you may recall, I have skills in graphic design and would be able to create new logo designs and write articles for the web site. I was pleased with your interest in my ideas for updating the web site. I know I can make a contribution to GoGardner.com while I learn as much as possible about the company and e-commerce.

Please let me know if I can provide you with any additional information about my qualifications or objectives. I look forward to hearing from you soon.

Sincerely,

Mary Going

A Note To Computer Animation Students

by Jenny Arata

I can organize just about anything, but don't judge that statement by the way my desk at home looks!

Several years ago at MetroLight Studios, the whole business of what to do with new demo reels was undecided. Who was to view them? Was there to be a hiring committee? When should the hiring committee meet? Should the reels be screened before the hiring committee met and who had time to do it? It was a mess. Not only that, but we had just come out of the most recent SIGGRAPH in Los Angeles, and we literally had hundreds of demo reels that languished in giant cartons waiting to be viewed. Part of the reason they had piled up unattended was because we'd had a change of employees in some job duties, and somehow the demo reels became neglected. What Metro Light desperately needed was for someone to simply say, "I'll be in charge." That part of me that is a glutton for punishment decided to rise to the challenge. I knew I could create a system for screening demo reels in a mostly timely fashion and for getting responses out to the animators. That was 1995. From that point on, I became the first contact for all demo reels.

A lot of demo reels have to be screened before gaining the experience to know what should be taken for further consideration and what should not pass beyond my office doors. I screened them, and I made the decision on who would go to the next level...the hiring committee. And so I began to pour through not only all those cases of demo reels from 1995 SIGGRAPH, but all the new ones that came in. I created a database that tells me not only the essential contact information but also what the animator's skills were, what he wanted to pursue, and some special note about the reel to trigger the memory of it in my mind. I began to campaign for some animators (including students) whose reels showed extraordinary talent, and many, but not all, of these people were hired. There are animators today that I am hoping to see hired by MetroLight, but if there aren't any openings and the timing isn't right, there's nothing I can do but wish the animator luck and try to keep in touch.

Jenny Arata joined Metro Light Studios in 1992 and among her many other duties reviews all demo reels and résumés. Also a screenwriter, her film, *The Thirteenth Year* plays regularly on The Disney Channel.

Metro Light Studios Inc. is a Los Angeles based Academy Award winning animation house specializing in high-end computer-generated imagery and digital special effects.

www.metrolight.com

Often, however, I see common mistakes that animators make because they are 1) in too much of a hurry to get their work out that they don't take the time to edit or animate with real care, or 2) they have totally mis-marketed their work (i.e. sending only traditional cell animation to a place that only does CGI).

"Do research and know what you're looking for — we look for people who really know what they want to do."
— Paula Fellbaum, recruiter,
        Mainframe Entertainment

There are many good resources available that will help the animators target their areas of interest if the animators will just take the time to use them. One of the best ways to know how to target the portfolio is to subscribe to magazines that are of interest (i.e., Computer Graphics World, 3D Magazine or 3D Artist). Each year these periodicals publish lists of companies, the strategies for hiring, and even what they want to see in demo reels. Every year The Hollywood Reporter also publishes a special issue on Careers in Animation and does the same thing. Animators should take advantage of SIGGRAPH, the Mecca of animation gatherings and make sure they pick up the specially tailored SIGGRAPH issue of The Hollywood Reporter and Daily Variety. There are literally thousands of companies (from 2500 employees worldwide with Walt Disney Feature Animation to two guys in a garage in Poughkeepsie) all over the world who are beating out a living as animators.

Internships
Not all animation houses provide internships, even if an animator promises to work for free! However, even if a company does offer an internship, the coveted spots are very few and even harder to get than an actual paying job in the industry!

Even the most well-done presentation, however, does not guarantee an internship position. There are few positions open and many people wanting to fill each spot. Not all studios even have an internship program, or if they do, the pay may be minimal to nothing. A lot of students are willing to work for free to get their foot in the door, but even a free worker still has to have computer skills and creativity shown in the presentation to make the company take the animator in-house.

If a prospective animation intern does not have a demo reel, they cannot get an internship at a digital animation house. The hiring company has to see proof of the ability to join the team, and the proof is on the demo reel. Based on the strength of a portfolio of artwork, it may be possible to get an internship at a traditional animation house, but that is up to the discretion of the company.

The intern must be literate and competent in at least one of the major animation software packages as well as understanding UNIX. The more the intern knows, the better. Someone who simply says, "I have no experience but I'm interested in this field," is not a good candidate for an internship.

Interns should follow submission procedures as if they were applying for a salaried position.

The Animator's Portfolio

The word portfolio comes from the Italian word, portfolio, which is most often used to mean "a portable case for holding papers, drawings, etc." While this definition applies to the physical artwork itself, a better, all encompassing definition is "an itemized list of investments or securities." The portfolio is the embodiment of the animator's art and becomes the very essence of the time, energy, and creative industry of the animator. That is why creating a portfolio presentation should be treated with great care.

The presentation of the portfolio has nothing to do with the outward appearance of the packaging or what expense was paid in shipping to get it more quickly into the hands of the prospective employer. In my years of screening demo reels, I can almost guarantee that an over-packaged demo reel or résumé is compensating for a lack of content. I've received reels that came in giant plastic cases, some are decorated elaborately, but these outward appearances are meaningless, especially when compared to the content. So I always advise animators not to put any extra time or effort into the beautifying of the external portfolio. The time is much better spent on the content.

Your portfolio is the first impression you will make on a prospective employer. Therefore, it is prudent to make the best impression possible.

The portfolio always includes:

1 Résumé

2 Demo reel

3 Demo reel log

4 Drawing/painting portfolio

The Résumé
(see sample at the end)

Keep your résumé as plain and to the point as possible by keeping all information easy to find at a glance (this includes having a legible and normal-sized font!). Demonstrating your designing ability by having an over-designed, "cute" résumé is a visual turn-off because it is generally difficult to read and pull out the pertinent information.

The following information should always be included:

1 Complete name, address, phone numbers and e-mail.

2 Practical professional experience only. If you worked for a firm that utilized your CGI knowledge or artistic capabilities, that's important.

3 Software knowledge and years spent with the software.

4 Hardware and operating systems knowledge.

5 Art/film school or university attended. Not a determining factor in hiring, however.

6 Relevant coursework.

Note: Always have someone proof-read your résumé for errors and general content.

The Demo Reel

At Metro Light Studios, we receive an average of 10 demo reels per week. That's approximately 520 per year, and then there are a couple hundred more added onto that from SIGGRAPH. Metro Light, on the other hand, hires only 1-2 animators per year, and that's if there is an opening, and if there is enough work to warrant hiring. Animators who are local with 2+ years of production experience get put into a database. There is a separate database for animators who are not local but who have excellent production experience. Animators who have superb demo reels but no production experience go into a database as someone that should be hired when they are available and when Metro Light has an opening. I stay in touch with entry level animators and have been able to push for many young talents to be hired at Metro Light, many of whom are still there. All other demo reels are sent to a plastics recycling plant. Sometimes a demo reel is returned if the animator has enclosed postage, but the animator shouldn't really worry about ever seeing the reel again. Give the demo reels away like candy. Send them out 4th class.

There's nothing I like better on a demo reel than an assembly of creativity that's animated excellently. You can't help but get good at understanding a good reel from one that still needs a lot of work when you've literally viewed thousands. When I started to see some problems with presentations and animations, I started to take notes and eventually compiled a list of basic do's and don'ts. In a recent article in the Hollywood Reporter, my colleagues in the industry concur on the major points.

Some will undoubtedly say that viewing a demo reel/portfolio and choosing whom to hire is subjectively based on the employer's tastes. I don't, however, subscribe to this philosophy. There have probably only been a very few of the many hundreds of reels I've screened that I rejected solely on their content. One was a supposed anti-rape public service announcement that let you see things through the eyes of a deranged rapist who was actively stalking his next victim. This missed the point entirely. Another reel that I rejected was full of sado-masochistic torture images, bloody skeletons and corpses in various stages of bondage and butchery. Although the animation was done well, and I did show it to a senior animator for a second opinion, we both agreed that we didn't want someone working for the company who spent time dreaming up images like that. So yes, it is slightly subjective based on personal taste.

Do not submit the demo reel on diskette, CD-ROM; point us to your website or attach zillions of still images to an e-mail to us. Send a demo reel if you are an animator. NTSC VHS or 3/4.

"Web sites and CD-ROMs are not recommended."
— Rachelle Meister, Director of Human Resources
Tippet Studio [2]

"We stay away from CD-ROMs and going to anybody's website."
— Patrick Kenney, Staff Development Manager
Will Vinton Studios [3]

"We don't encourage people to send in discs or CD-ROMs..."
— Rachel Hannah, Recruiting Manager
Pixar Animation Studios [4]

The demo reel is the animator's showpiece. It contains examples of completed animation sequences (computer animation, traditional animation, claymation/stop-motion), animation tests (includes pencil tests, wire-frames), and works in progress, and it can even include still images of art work. When a reel is well-edited, these things flow seamlessly together, but when the animator has spent no time in editing and the pieces are simply tacked together (and sometimes repeated to give the reel length!) then the reel is less interesting.

"As far as presentation, keep the reels short. Put only the best work on them. And always let us know what you were responsible for in the scenes you chose."
— Blue Sky Studios [5]

"The reel should represent the work you're most proud of with the most recent work first. Keep it short…"
— Beth Sasseen, Digital Relations Project Manager
Industrial Light and Magic [6]

Although which software you know might be important, how well you know and manipulate it is of greater value. And what have you done creatively with it?

Demo reels and résumés have been known to get separated, so make sure the demo has all contact information on it .

"…give us full contact information. You'd be surprised how hard it is to get in touch with artists we're interested in sometimes."
— Jeff Fino, Partner
Wild Brain [7]

While I cannot tell you what to put on your reel, I can say that it's important to make an impression. It is always nice to see spoofs of products or commercials. Anything that tells a short story and makes us laugh is good. Works in progress are okay as long as you label it so and even explain what you'd like to do with it.

I see a lot of the exact same classroom exercises on student demo reels, and the impression that leaves me with immediately is "this person isn't ready." It's actually a little annoying to sit through those. Don't put classroom exercises on your demo reel, no matter how well you accomplished it! Leave it in the classroom-and that includes the following:

1 Simple stick figures doing a walking/running test in place. If they've got to walk, dress them up a bit and make them walk somewhere.

2 Bouncing balls and boxes. Most of these animations have the ball or box warp its shape in order to make the maneuver, and that looks cheesy. Good lighting, shading and sound effects without the warping accomplish the task much better.

3   Simple bugs. These are extremely simplistic animations that look plastic and the movements cause the joints to disappear into other parts of the body. A stylized plastic look is great, but this is inexperience.

4   Simple robots. The robots generally come from the male animators, and what applies to simple bugs applies here too.

5   Simple spaceships. Space and space ships, also very commonly animated, must be fairly easy to do because they are so common, and undoubtedly these are made with the hope that George Lucas may one day see it and say, "You must come work on my next Star Wars epic!" But these are so common as to be blasé.

Focus more on developing the following:

1   Natural phenomenon (includes snow, clouds, water, fire, etc.)

2   Sophisticated imagery animation (includes creatures, characters, cars, mattes, objects)

Make certain your camera moves are smooth and your lighting is consistent. Do not repeat the works on your demo reel simply to make it longer. Music helps. A silent reel is boring. Edit. Edit. Edit! Color bars and tone are never necessary.

Note: Flip books are not acceptable as a substitute for a demo reel although they may be included as an overall part of the portfolio submission. However, they count little to nothing towards hiring and are considered more of a novelty than hands-on animation.

Demo Reel Log
(see sample)

Always include a log of what is on the demo reel and specify exactly what you did on the animations. If more than one person worked on a specific piece, be sure to say which part of the piece you did.

"We really want to see a concise reel that shows best work. And we need to know what exactly an applicant has done on the reel."
— Jamie Toscas, Recruiting
Dream Quest Images [8]

"The reel should be clearly labeled and include a log that identifies the artist's role in each piece."
— Alison Dexter, Sr. VP of Production and Operations
Nickelodeon Animation Studios, New York [9]

Artwork Portfolio

As a general rule, never send original artwork. Always send pictures of the artwork only. This can mean a color printout, by the way, and certainly any image that is sent should be large enough and clear enough for the employer to get a really good idea about the artist. If you are called in for an interview, you can always bring in the original pieces at that time.

Do not include copies of your drawings, sketches, etc., when applying for a computer animator position. You may, however, bring them to the interview as well as mention that you have a portfolio.

The artwork portfolio is more applicable to a traditional animation job or to an art director staff position.

"The thing that's looked for most is that someone can draw. We always want to see good composition and good structure in characters. For storyboard artists and directors, we want to see that they know how to stage things in interesting ways, and that they know how to construct a story."
— Marge Dean, Director of Animation Production
Sony Pictures Family Entertainment [10]

Shipping

Demo reels should not be shipped unprotected. Keep them in the protective case they came in or buy the very inexpensive plastic ones. Too many reels arrive smashed by the postal system when unprotected. Blank 10 minute tapes can be purchased from a supplier for about $1 each, hard plastic cases run about $1.50 each, and cardboard cases at about .05 each. First class mail should be less than $2 within the USA. Reels going out of the USA or coming into the USA will have to pay customs.

Send demo reels in bubble-padded envelopes, not jiffy bags (envelopes padded with pulp paper) and not the cardboard priority mail envelope (very smashable). Jiffy bags burst and can ruin your demo reel by infesting it with the pulp and dust of its padding. Your post office should have bubble bags and if not, check with your local office supply store. I recommend the #1 size.

Don't overdo the packaging. Expensive packaging isn't necessary, and it doesn't impress anyone. It ends up in the trash or recycle bin along with the cheap packaging. Unless specifically requested to do so, do not send the demo reels UPS, FEDEX, certified or anything else that is an extra expense. Save yourself the money and just send things regular mail. You may feel an urgency to send out your reel, but on the receiving end, there's no urgency.

After the information has been sent:
Don't badger the company as to whether or not they've received your résumé and/or demo reel. Even if you think you're being polite in making an inquiry, it feels like badgering. If the company is interested, you will be contacted for an interview. If not, you might receive a written notice. Some companies return demo reels and some do not. If you specifically wish for the return of your demo, enclose a self-addressed stamped envelope (padded, of course). NEVER send your **only** demo reel. Always make a dub.

In Conclusion
Although software knowledge is important, I cannot stress enough how much more we and our competitors look for creative talent above all. We know that students often do not have access to the high-end software packages or to the proper resources. That is why it is extremely important to become very proficient on the software you can get hold of.

I hope this helps, and the best of luck to everyone!

— Jenny Arata

Résumé Sample

Chris Jones
123 Main Street
Anytown USA 55555
(555) 555-5555

E-mail: chris@anywhere.com
URL: http://www.anything.com

Experience
(Include practical professional experience only. If you worked for a firm that utilized your CGI knowledge or artistic capabilities, that's important.)

Yapping Pup Productions - June 1998 - Feb. 1999. Technical director. Worked on corporate logos including "WCAT" in Baton Rouge, and "Here's Your Mattress" for The Mattress Warehouse in Murfreesboro.

Software Knowledge
(List software in order of most knowledge and experience. Don't oversell yourself on something you think human resource people want to see here. We can tell by the demo reel.)

Lightwave (2 yrs), Composer (6 mo's), Adobe Illustrator (1 yr), Adobe (learning), Windows NT, Mac OS, some

Hardware Experience
Mac, PC, SGI (in school) and Unix (in school).

Education
School of Animation and Art, Any City - graduated 1998
State College or University, Any City - attended 1992-1994

Relevant Coursework
1 semester CAD, 2 semesters shell scripting in C++, 2 years Light wave training. 8 semesters traditional painting, 8 semesters computer animation, 6 semesters traditional cell animation.

Other
I own a PC and love coming up with my own animation. I am currently working on a 30-minute 3D animation about snowboarding which I have scripted and storyboarded.

Demo Log Sample
(This needs to be included INSIDE the demo reel case or cardboard cover.)

CHRIS JONES
123 Main Street
Anytown USA
800-555-1212

Opening Logo
WVVW Logo - Turkey Jerky Advertising
girl on balance beam
asteroids and spaceships colliding
avalanche
snowboarding animation (in progress)
traditional animation pencil test
still photographs
paintings
closing logo

NOTE: All animation was done by me in Lightwave and Wavefront
Composer except for the WVVW logo which was done by myself and 2
other animators. On that job I handled all the modeling and lighting.

[1]The Hollywood Reporter - "Careers in Animation Special Issue." October 22, 1999. pg. S-8; 2 Ibid pg. S-9; 3Ibid pg. S-9; 4 Ibid pg. S-9; 5 Ibid pg. S-7; 6 Ibid pg. S-8; 7 Ibid pg. S-9; 8 Ibid pg. S-8; 9 Ibid pg. S-6; 10 Ibid pg. S-7

Internship Organizations

The Washington Center for Internships

The Washington Center is a not-for-profit internship placement organization that assists students of participating colleges and universities in locating internships in the Washington DC area. Internship for new media individuals can work on stations such as CNN and on programs such as *Larry King Live*. The organization works with over 400 interns applicants each term. The Washington Center reviews each candidate for the main internship program on an individual basis and accepts qualified applicants on the basis of the eligibility criteria. Undergraduate and graduate students of any major and discipline are eligible to apply. To be considered for the main internship program, the student must:

- Be enrolled at an accredited college or university.

- Be a second semester sophomore or above at the time of the internship.

- Maintain a 2.5 G.P.A. (minimum 3.0 G.P.A.. is required for federal agencies such as the Departments of Commerce, Interior, Justice, State, and Treasury, the United States Attorney's Office and the Cable News Network (CNN)).

- Receive academic credit from the college or university for the student participation.

- Receive the endorsement of the campus liaison or faculty sponsor.

International students to the program

According to the Washington Center for Internships, international students attending colleges and universities in the US are eligible to apply through the campus liaison. Those attending institutions abroad not affiliated with The Washington Center may apply if able to obtain an appropriate visa or visa waiver. The Washington Center does not issue visas. For short-term, three-month internships, international students should contact the Center's international program partner, CDS International, at http://www.cdsintl.org for further information.

Application requirements

To participate in this year round program students must submit an application, essay, letter of recommendation and transcript with a $60 application fee.

Deadline

Deadline varies from program to program and depending on whether clearance is needed for the position. Internship programs last from 10-12 weeks.

Contact

The Washington Center for Internships
1101 14th Street NW, Suite 500, Washington, DC 20005
Phone: 202-336-7600
800-486-8921
Fax: 202-336-7609
URL: http://www.twc.edu

Knight Ridder Specialty Development Program

This program is designed to bring minority voices into newsrooms in areas where minorities have not traditionally been well represented. Knight Ridder specialist trainees have been hired into photography, design, arts criticism, business writing and computer assisted or new media journalism. The program is not meant to train people for areas where minority journalists are beginning to be represented. The strategy is to find high-potential people who have demonstrated through their work or academics an interest in a journalistic specialty, and to put them to work with people who will train, coach and advise them in that specialty. They choose people only for areas in which the company feels it has the ability to do meaningful training. One feature of the program is some specialized training at an off-site seminar. Previous participants have attended National Writers' Workshops and photography seminars.

Knight Ridder editors will work with the intern graduates as they continue their careers after that first year, either at the paper they started with or, if possible, another Knight Ridder newspaper. It is certainly Knight Ridder's intent to develop minority specialists for its newsrooms, but there is no obligation — on Knight Ridder or the journalist — to continue the relationship. Most KR specialty alumni are working at Knight Ridder newsrooms, and all but one are working as journalists.

Application Requirements
Résumé
Six clips for writers, artists, designers;
20 images for photographers
A cover letter
A four-page professional essay describing the student's interest and development in journalism, including key influences and plans
The names of three references to be contacted (letters are not necessary.)

Deadline
Materials must be received by Dec. 1.

Knight Ridder Contacts

Corporate
Knight Ridder, Inc.
One Herald Plaza
Miami, FL 33132-1693
305-376-3800
Contact:
Becky Baybrook-Heckenbach

Daily Newspapers
Aberdeen American News
124 South Second Street
Aberdeen, SD 57401
Phone: 605-225-4100
Contact: Executive Editor
Cindy Eikamp

Akron Beacon Journal
44 East Exchange Street
Akron, OH 44328
Phone: 330-996-3708
Contact: Manager of Recruiting
and Development
Crystal Williams

(Antioch, Calif.) Ledger Dispatch
1650 Cavallo Road
Antioch, CA 94509
Phone: 510-757-2525
Contact: Administrative Assistant
Deborah Mathias

The (Belleville, Ill.)
News-Democrat
120 S. Illinois St.
Belleville, IL 62222
Phone: 618-234-1000
Contact: Sports Editor
Joseph Ostermeier

The (Biloxi) Sun Herald
205 DeBuys Road
Gulfport, MS 39507
Phone: 601-896-2100
Contact: Staff Reporter
Don Adderton

Bradenton Herald
102 Manatee Avenue West
Bradenton, FL 34205
Phone: 941-748-0411
Contacts: HR Director
Barbara Cashion
Executive Editor
Wayne Poston

The Charlotte Observer
600 South Tryon Street
Charlotte, NC 28202
Phone: 704-358-5000
Contact: Sr. Editor/Staff
Development Jim Walser
jwalser@aol.com

The (Columbia) State
1401 Shop Street
Columbia, SC 29201
Phone: 803-771-6161
Contacts: HR Director
Holly Rogers
Asst. to Managing Editor
Beverly Dominick

Columbus Ledger-Enquirer
17 West 12th Street
Columbus, GA 31901
Phone: 706-324-5526
Contact: Executive Editor
Mike Burbach

Contra Costa (Calif.) Times
2640 Shadelands Drive
Walnut Creek, CA 94596
Phone: 925-935-2525
Contacts: Managing Editor
Saundra Keyes
skeyes@cctimes.com
Operations Director/HR
Laurie Fox

Detroit Free Press
600 W. Fort Street
Detroit, MI 48226
Phone: 800-678-6400. ext. 6490
Contact: Recruiting &
Development Editor
Joe Grimm
grimm@det-freepress.com

The Duluth News-Tribune
424 West First Street
Duluth, MN 55802
Phone: 218-723-5281
Contacts: Executive Editor
Vickie Gowler
Intern Coordinator
Holly Gruber

The (Fort Wayne) News-Sentinel
600 West Main Street
Fort Wayne, IN 46802
Phone: 219-461-8444
Contact: Managing Editor
Carolyn Di Paolo

The Fort Worth Star-Telegram
400 W. 7th St.
Fort Worth, TX 76101
Phone: 817-390-7831
Contacts: Busienss editor
Liz Zavala

Grand Forks Herald
303 Second Avenue
Grand Forks, ND 58203
Phone: 701-780-1100
Contact: Managing Editor/
Administration
Greg Turosak

Kansas City Star
1729 Grand Blvd.
Kansas City, MO 64108
Phone: 816-234-4884
Contact: Yvette Walker

Lexington Herald-Leader
100 Midland Avenue
Lexington, KY 40508
Phone: 606-231-3100
Contact: Asst. Managing Editor
Mike Johnson

The Macon Telegraph
120 Broadway
Macon, GA 31201-3444
Phone: 912-744-4200
Contact: Asst. to the Editor
Charles Richardson

The Miami Herald
One Herald Plaza
Miami, FL 33132-1693
Phone: 305-376-3558
Contacts: Ritu Sehgal for
newsroom jobs,
Natalie Williams for other jobs

El Nuevo (Miami) Herald
One Herald Plaza
Miami, FL 33132-1693
Phone: 305-376-3535
Contact: Executive Editor
Barbara Gutierrez

The Monterey County Herald
PO Box 271
Monterey, CA 93942-0271
Phone: 831-646-4342
Contact: Executive Editor
Peter S. Young

The (Myrtle Beach) Sun News
Frontage Road East
Myrtle Beach, SC 29577
Phone: 803-626-8555
Contact: Deputy Managing Editor
Gwen Fowler

Philadelphia Inquirer
400 N. Broad Street
Philadelphia, PA 19130
Phone: 215-854-4757
Contact: Sherry Howard

Philadelphia Daily News
400 North Broad St.
Philadelphia, PA 19130
Phone: 215-854-2000
Contact: Asst. Managing Editor
Mike Days

Saint Paul Pioneer Press
345 Cedar Street
St. Paul, MN 55101
Phone: 612-222-5011
Contact: VP/HR
Jill Taylor

San Jose Mercury News
750 Ridder Park Drive
San Jose, CA 95190
Phone: 408-920-5000
Contact: Asst. Managing Editor for
Features and
Development
Pat Thompson

(San Luis Obispo)
Telegram-Tribune
3825 S. Higuera
San Luis Obispo, CA 93406-0112
Phone: 805-781-7870
Contact: Editor
Jeff Fairbanks

San Ramon Valley Times
524 Hartz Avenue
Danville, CA 94526
Phone: 510-837-4267
Contact: Operations Director/HR
Laurie Fox

(State College) Centre Daily Times
3400 East College Avenue
State College, PA 16801
Phone: 814-231-4621
Contact: HR Director
Darlene Weener

Tallahassee Democrat
277 North Magnolia Drive
Tallahassee, FL 32301-2695
Phone: 904-599-2100
Contacts: Employment Services
Administrator
Cordelia Leon
Recruiter/Team leader
Janie Nelson

(Pleasanton, Calif.) Valley Times
127 Spring Street
Pleasanton, CA 94566
Phone: 510-462-4160
Contact: HR Representatives
Kathy Fingh and Shawn Leavitt

The Warner Robins (Ga.)
Daily News
1553 Watson Blvd.
Warner Robins, GA 31095
Phone: 912-328-7682
Contact: Managing editor
Robin Booken

(Richmond, Calif.)
West County Times
4301 Lakeside Drive
Richmond, CA 94806
Phone: 510-758-8400
Contact: Managing Editor
Anthony Marquez

The Wichita Eagle
825 East Douglas Ave.
Wichita, KS 67202
Phone: 316-268-6000
Contact: Neighbors Editor & Asst.
to Executive Editor
Fran Kentling

The (Wilkes-Barre, Pa.)
Times Leader
15 N. Main St.
Wilkes-Barre, PA 18711
Phone: 717-829-7100
Contact: Features Editor
Chris Ritchie

New Ventures

Knight Ridder New Media Center
981 Ridder Park Drive
San Jose, CA 95131
Phone: 408-467-1400
Contact: Editorial Director/New
Media David Yarnold

Mercury Center
750 Ridder Park Drive
San Jose, CA 95131
Phone: 408-920-5200
Contact: Managing Editor
Bruce Koon

Washington Offices

Knight Ridder/Tribune
Information Services
790 National Press Building
Washington, DC 20045
Phone: 800-435-7578
Contact: Jane Scholz, editor

Knight Ridder Washington Bureau
700 National Press Building
Washington, DC 20045
Phone: 202-383-6058
Contact: Clark Hoyt, editor

Internship
Profiles

1492 Pictures

General Information

The company consists of director Chris Columbus' (Home Alone, Mrs. Doubtfire, Nine Months, Stepmom) feature film and television production company at 20th Century Fox Studios.

Internships Available

Interns participate in all areas of feature film and television development by reading scripts and coverage, assisting in research, attending staff meetings and providing office support. Interns also review scripts, book reviews, and other media for potential projects and attend and report on student, festival, and special industry film screenings.

Benefits

This is a non-paid internship for academic credit only.

Contact

Lesley Howard
1492 Pictures
10201 W. Pico Blvd.
Building 86, Room 203
Los Angeles, CA 90035

Fax: 310-369-4743
E-mail: lesleyh@fox.com

Academy of Television Arts & Sciences

General Information

The Television Academy's internships have been designed to provide qualified full-time college and university graduate and undergraduate students (and students who have recently graduated) with in-depth exposure to professional television production facilities, techniques, and practices. The nationwide competition is highly competitive. Last year, out of approximately 1,000 applicants, 28 were selected. The Princeton Review has recognized the

Television Academy's competition as one of the top ten internship programs of any kind in the United States.

Internships Available

Internships exist in 27 categories: Agency, Animation-Traditional, Animation-Non-Traditional (computer generated), Art Direction, Broadcast Advertising and Promotion, Business Affairs, Casting, Children's Programming/Development, Cinematography, Commercials, Costume Design, Development, Documentary/Reality Production, Editing, Entertainment News, Episodic Series, Movies for Television, Music, Network Programming Management, Production Management, Public Relations and Publicity, Sound, Syndication/Distribution, Television Directing/Single Camera, Television Directing/Multi-Camera, Television Script Writing, and Videotape Post Production.

The official internship information flyer for the Summer 2000 program will be available on the web site. Flyers are also mailed to Career Resource Centers and TV/Film Departments nationwide. Please check these locations first. Locate the flyer by mid-January, or call the office and have one sent. Each applicant must follow the instructions on the current flyer as some entry requirements are revised from year to year. This flyer outlines exactly what materials must be submitted in order to be considered. (Note: there is no "application form" to fill out.)

Benefits

All internships are located in the Los Angeles area. Most internships begin during mid to late June or early July depending on the schedule of the company which hosts the internship. Each internship ends 8 weeks after the start date. (The Music category, however, normally starts in late July or August.) All positions are full-time. Each intern receives a stipend of $2,000. Interns whose permanent residence is outside Los Angeles County will receive an additional $400 to help defray travel/housing expenses.

Contact
Summer Student Internship Program
Academy of Television Arts & Sciences
Internship Program
5220 Lankershim Blvd.
North Hollywood,
CA 91601-3109

Phone: 818-754-2830
Fax: 818-761-2827
E-mail: internships@emmys.org.
URL: http://www.emmys.org

AIDS Walk San Francisco

General Information
AIDS Walk San Francisco is a Northern California AIDS fund-raising event. Over the past 12 years, unprecedented numbers of participants have raised more than $28 million in the fight to end AIDS.

Internships Available
Media/Community Organizer Intern—AIDS Walk San Francisco seeks interns for its various departments, including media and community organizing. Responsibilities include organizing volunteer activities, proofing various print material, assisting the event manager, tracking media relations, and working with the corporate and community team coordination efforts. Interns also work at the event. Interns should be industrious, and willing to work some weekends or evenings, and committed to grassroots fund-raising organization and AIDS awareness issues. This is an opportunity to learn about all aspects of grassroots fund-raising and event planning.

Benefits
Unpaid internship.

Contact
Mona Abdallah
AIDS Walk
230 California Street, Suite 400
San Francisco, California, 94111

Phone: 415-392-9255
Fax: 415-392-8707
E-mail: msabdallah@compuserve.com
URL: http://www.aidswalk.net

American Association of School Administrators

General Information

Founded in 1865, AASA's mission is to support and develop effective school system leaders who are dedicated to the highest quality public education for all children. The four major focus areas for AASA are: Improving the condition of children and youth; Preparing schools and school systems for the 21st century; Connecting schools and communities; Enhancing the quality and effectiveness of school leaders.

Internship Available

Various teaching opportunities are available in the area of computer technology. Web intern—responsible for assisting with basic HTML coding and writing basic summaries for the web site. Working on an on-line resource catalog that provides an array of titles from Corwin Press, Jossey-Bass, Educational Research Service, Technomics Publishing and more.

Benefits

Offers on-the-job training. College credit possibilities. Unpaid internship.

Contact

Liz Griffin
American Association of School Administrators
1801 North Moore Street
Arlington, VA 22209

Phone: 703-528-0700
fax: 703-841-1543
http://www.aasa.org

American Training of Massachusetts

General Information

Human Service Agency encourages all individuals, no matter what disadvantage they may have, to challenge themselves to meet the maximum of their abilities. American Training, advocates for the respect and dignity that every person is entitled to. The people they support are taught to advocate for themselves. Individuals are encouraged to make quantitative choices which will afford meaningful work, living arrangements, and relationships within the community.

Internships Available

Graphic designer—design eye catching brochures, flyers, and posters for a nonprofit human service agency.

Benefits

Work from home if desired. Time frames are flexible. Unpaid internship. Skills: computer training, graphic design

Contact

Michelle LaFay
American Training of Massachusetts
102 Glenn Street
Lawrence, Massachusetts, 01843

Phone: 978-685-2151
Fax: 978-683-5124
E-mail: MLAFAY2258@aol.com

Amp NYC Animation

General Information

A New York-based studio that provides a mix of digital technology with time-honored animation techniques. The studio's production team has created work for clients such as MTV, Primestar Satellite Television, Showtime Channel, and the Cartoon Network. AMP's work for the Cartoon Network was honored to receive the ASIFA East Award for Best Direction for Spots Under Two Minutes also the 1997 Promax/ Broadcast Design Awards' Gold Medal for Cel Animation and Bronze Medal for Spots Over Ten Seconds.

Internships Available

Internships are available in various aspects of animation production and post-production.

Benefits:

Contact the company for more information.

Contact

Amp NYC Animation
250 Fifth Ave., Ste. 400
New York, NY 10001

Phone: 310-550-5826
Fax: 212-213-3869
E-mail: ampnyc@aol.com

Anchorage Daily News

General Information: Established in 1946, 530 employees work on the daily newspapers.

Internship Available

Intern positions include reporters, photographers, copy editors and graphic artists. Reporting and photography interns work on general assignment news and features. Editors are on the main news copy desk. Artists produce news graphics. The Daily News works with students to enhance their portfolios.

Benefits

Interns will participate in weekly lunch-and-learn sessions on newspaper journalism issues and practices. Interns earn $9.50 an hour for a 40-hour week. Each internship lasts for 12 weeks. Reporting and photography interns must have a valid driver's license and must provide their own insured vehicle.

Contact
News Internship Coordinator
c/o Human Resources
Anchorage Daily News
P.O. Box 149001
Anchorage, AK 99514-9001

Fax: 907-257-4472 (Attn.: Human Resources)
E-mail: jobs@adn.com
URL: http://www.adn.com

Animate NYC

General Information

A script to screen creative services company. The company develops original characters, scripts, storyboards and programming for feature film, TV series and digital media. Specializes in multiple mediums combining 2D, 3D, clay animation, digital stop motion and special effects.

Internships Available

Internships are arranged with two months advance notice. Various possibilities.

Benefits

Unpaid with opportunity for college credits.

Contact
Animate NYC
44 W. 24th St.
New York, NY 10010

Phone: 917-854-1176
Fax: 212-229-0237
E-mail: animatenyc@aol.com
Web Address: http://www.animationnyc.com

Aperture Foundation

General Information

A not-for-profit organization for the promotion of photography through published books, exhibitions and educational programs.

Internships Available

Various internships are available in several different areas. Multimedia internships in the area of design—responsibilities include preparing files for color output, creating mechanicals, sizing art, scanning and placing photographs, conceptual design on selected projects, and general office support.

Benefits

Paid interns receive $250 per month in addition to college credit.

Contact

Maris Desey
Work-Scholar Coordinator
Aperture Foundation
20 East 23rd Street
New York, NY 10010

Phone: 212-505-5555
Fax: 212-979-7759
E-mail: mdecsey@aperture.org
URL: http://www.aperture.org

Archive Films/Archive Photos

General Information

Archive Films/Archive Photos is a stock image/content provider company which currently has 125 employees.

Internship Available

Archive Films/Archive Photos has an active intern program for college students and recent graduates looking to gain experience in the stock image business. Internships are available in the areas of film research, film acquisition, digital imaging, photo librarian, and photo research.

Benefits

These are short-term non-paid positions; students may be able to receive course credits.

Contact

Human Resources
Archive Films/Archive Photos
530 W. 25th Street
New York, NY 10001

Fax: 212-822-7857.
URL: http://www.archivefilms.com

The Arkansas Educational Telecommunications Network

General Information

The Arkansas Educational Telecommunications Network is a public television network

Internships Available: Variety of internship opportunities available in several departments. Internships are open to students thinking about a career in Public Television.

Communications Department—*Outreach/Publicist Intern* (10-15 flexible hours a week) Research; Write programming features and news/press releases; Call the statewide newspapers and develop working relationships with editors; Prepare and mail outreach information packets; Additional duties as needed. *Program Guide Intern* (6-10 flexible hours a week) Programming research for AETN's monthly Program Guide, includes searching for program titles, photos and show descriptions; layout and design for Program Guide, new-print and magazine advertising; layout and design for brochures, flyers and newsletters; Works with designer to design, build, paint and assemble AETN production sets; Set up a filing system for AETN's color slide photography; illustration, light filing, research and writing.

Operations Department—*Administrative Intern* (10-15 flexible hours a week) Assist Director of Operations or Facilities Coordinator with written correspondence, scheduling, telephone calls and reports. Intern would also schedule state vehicles and assist in the record keeping in this department. *Field/Studio Intern* (10-15 flexible hours a week) Opportunity to work and train in the following areas: lighting; setting up sets and props; assist in directing and floor directing; teleprompter operation; Studio camera work; assist videographers on remote shoots; assist in the editing process.

Production Department—*Production Intern* (10-15 flexible hours a week) Assist in general office duties in the following areas: answer routine viewer calls; screen and transcribe videotapes; assist various producers in preparing programs for broadcast, including setting up interviews, researching background; material for scripts, transcribing video, program development and preparing FCC reports; assist producers with phone supervision during live broadcasts, including greeting guests at the front door, escorting them to the proper area, answering phones, collecting questions and handling other requests made by the phone supervisor. Interns in this area will complete their internship by preparing a 30-second program promo for statewide broadcast. Working with a production supervisor, the intern will develop the promo concept; prepare the outline, script and storyboard; select music and video for completion. Final editing of the project would take place on an AVID editing system. The intern supervises the editing process.

Benefits

Student interns experience first-hand the operations of a local PBS broadcast facility. Supervisors are flexible and work with students according to each student's schedule, experience and internship requirements. The intern position is non-paid, therefore, AETN understands the need for outside employment and works to accommodate individual work schedules. Unpaid internships for college credits or other arrangements.

Contact
Martha Perry
Intern Coordinator
AETN
P.O. Box 1250
Conway, AR 72033

Phone: 800-662-2386
E-mail: mperry@aetn.org
URL: http://www.aetn.org

Artbear Pigmation, Inc.

General Information

Artbear Pigmation has been producing animation, from concept through final output for the past 27 years. Specializing in character design, project development, and animation creating combinations of live action, 3D, and/or photo collage with traditional characters. The company produces shorts on video and film for the purposes of educational, instructional videos or television commercials.

Internship Available

Both traditional and computer animation positions are available at this studio.

Benefits

Unpaid internships. College credits.

Contact

Artbear Pigmation, Inc.
415 Elm Street
Ithaca, NY 14850

Phone: 607-277-1151
Fax: 607-277-1166
E-mail: artbear@clarityconnect.com
URL: http://people.clarityconnect.com/webpages/artbear/artbear.html

Arts & Education Corporation

General Information

Sponsorship of educational and cultural programs, Arts & Education Corporation produces socially responsible multimedia programming. Area of Focus: Education, Foundations and Fund-raising Coalitions, Media.

Internships Available

Associate Producer—coordinate video production distribution, identify new socially responsible video projects. Background in sales, fund-raising and public relations helpful.

Benefits

Unpaid internship

Contact

Dale Orlando
Arts & Education Corporation
101 Atlantic Ave.
Marblehead, Massachusetts, 01945

Phone: 781-581-3029
Fax: 781-593-6678
E-mail: arts@newenglandusa.com
URL: http://newenglandusa.com/Arts_Ed/arts_ed.html

Association for Independent Video & Filmmakers

General Information

AIVF is the national service organization for independent media providing programs and services, as well as a sense of community. AIVF is also an information clearinghouse —publishing a national magazine and several books, maintaining a library of media arts resources, and sponsoring events throughout the country.

Internship Available

Individuals interested or involved in media arts and independent film/video work directly with AIVF staff in the SoHo office environment. AIVF offers interns flexible scheduling, hands-on learning experience, and prime exposure to the vast independent filmmaking community. For those looking to move into film or video production, being actively involved with AIVF has information resources and connections to further develop careers. AIVF interns: assist Information Services Director with Resource Library organization and upkeep, including updating resource binders and handouts, and assisting with development of comprehensive reference lists; assist Membership department with monthly renewal mailings and database maintenance; assist Information Services Director with upkeep of Festival, Distributor, and Exhibitor Databases and revisions to new book editions; Answer phones and respond to information requests; coordinate bulletin boards and résumé banks in Resource Library; fulfill book orders, complete invoices, and maintain database and inventory records; maintain mailing lists as directed by Membership department; check general voice mailbox, Events RSVP, and Book Order Hotline on a regular basis and respond accordingly.

Benefits

Unpaid internships.

Contact
Association for Independent Video & Filmmakers
(also the Foundation for Independent Video and Film)
304 Hudson Street, 6th floor
New York, NY 10013

Phone: 212-807-1400
Fax: 212-463-8519
E-mail: info@aivf.org
URL: http://www.aivf.org

Baltimore Magazine

General Information

Baltimore Magazine offers internships to anyone currently enrolled in a college
or university undergraduate or graduate program.

Internships Available

Internships for spring, summer, fall, and winter semesters for journalism,
photography, graphic design, and advertising/marketing.

Benefits

Unpaid internship. Students must be eligible to receive credit to be considered
and must commit to at least 16 hours per week (editorial requirement only).

Contact

Georgia Hurff, Research Director
Tabitha Wilson, Art Director
David Colwell, Dir. of Photography or
Jenny Bishop, Dir. of Advertising
Baltimore Magazine
1000 Lancaster St., Suite 400
Baltimore, Maryland 21202

Fax: 410-625-0280
Editorial Department
E-mail: lcath@baltimoremag.com

Art & Design / Production Department
E-mail: wamanda@baltimoremag.com

Photography Department
E-mail: cdavid@baltimoremag.com

URL: http://www.baltimoremag.com/

The Bakersfield Californian

General Information
The Bakersfield Californian is an independent, family-owned newspaper. It is the direct descendent of Kern County's first newspaper, The Weekly Courier, which was first published Aug. 18, 1866, in Havilah, Calif. Today it employs over 380.

Internship Available
The Bakersfield Californian has a year-round internship program with eight positions — four in reporting and four in photography.

Benefits
Each is a 13-week-long, full-time internship paying $340 per week ($8.50 per hour). The company will supply cars for reporters and photographers sent out on assignment; however, interns must have means of transportation to and from work. Assistance is available to find affordable lodging; the intern is responsible for making his or her own living arrangements.

Contact
Casey Christie
Director of Photography or
Felix Adamo, Asst. Director of Photography
The Bakersfield Californian
P.O. Box 440
Bakersfield, CA 93302

Phone: 661-395-7500
URL: http://www.bakersfield.com

BNN

General Information

A Time Warner's New York Cable News service. Established in 1983, BNN has produced for VH1, Disney, The Travel Channel, NBC, the ASPCA and Scholastic. Currently development in web design and deployment, video journalism, comedy, feature films, and all manner of human expression. BNN is a television production and program development facility located in New York, NY. BNN has produced program segments for clients including: MTV, CBS, A&E, VH1, Court TV, The Sci-Fi Channel, Lifetime, Fox Television, ABC, NBC, ESPN, The Today Show, MacNeil-Lehrer Newshour, Entertainment Tonight, Travel Channel and BRAVO.

Internships Available

Internships are intensive hands-on opportunities in documentary and series television production. Interns work both in the field and in the facility. Often interns work with documentary producers in the process of research, shooting, writing, and post-production of finished films. Various options for an internship. A *Production/Creative Internship* involves all programming in development and production. Research, both on the web and in the library. Phone calls. Assisting the associate producer. Transcribing tape. Assisting the producer during the edit. And show wrap up. Internship is a track to becoming a Producer or Video journalist. A *Tech/Ops Internship* involves working closely with the technical department assisting with hooking up equipment, digitizing into the AVID, preparing camera kits, troubleshooting computer problems, and media management. Internship is a track to Technical Engineer or Facility Management. The *Marketing/Sales Internship* involves working with the Director of Marketing and Sales, creating and sending out press packets, contacting various media about their programs, research, building databases, event planning. Creating a presence at various conferences like MIP.com and NAPTE. The *New Media Internship* involves working with QuickTime/RealVideo streaming of video and audio, bulletin boards, website building and maintenance, entry, troubleshooting as well as research of new web and video technologies. BNN accommodates 10-15 interns per session.

Benefits
Interns take part in production. No monetary compensation for the learning experience. Students earn credit if arranged in advance.

Contact
URL: http://www.bnntv.com
E-mail: steve@broadcastnews.com

Buzzco Associates, Inc.

General Information
Buzzco Associates is a traditional animation house that has created animation shorts and ID spots for such clients as Nickelodeon, Burger King and several others. Since 1987 the company have created 6 shorts and several commercial projects. The company consists of 5 employees.

Internship Available
The number of positions, projects and duration varies with the individual students and work flow in the studio. Interns at Buzzco Associates often work for the duration range of 6 weeks to 6 months (with a minimum of 3 days and/or 20 hours per week) and responsibilities have ranged from film editorial experience, production assistance, and research along with messaging. In return, there has been time and facilities (and guidance) on individual projects.

Benefits
This is an unpaid internship.

Contact
Buzzco Associates, Inc.
33 Bleecker Street
New York, NY 10012

Phone: 212-473-8800
Fax: 212-473-8891
E-mail: Info@buzzzco.com
URL: http://www.buzzzco.com

ByLandSeaAndAir.Com

General Information

BylandSeaAndAir.com is a new Internet start-up that caters to Zoo, Aquarium and nature enthusiasts. The clientele includes children, college students, adults and families. It is a virtual organization and has employees in the Midwest and New England.

Internships Available

Internships are available in the following areas: Marketing, Public Relations, Web Design, Human Resources, Writers, Zoology and Marine majors, Accounting/Finance, Information Technology. Interns must be located in the USA, Internet/Computer literate, in college with a G.P.A. over 2.5. In addition, interns must have access to a computer and a modem, and have working knowledge of Microsoft Office Suite. Interns must be able to work 5 to 10 hours a week, with a choice of days, nights or weekends.

Benefits

These are nonpaying internships. First Come First Served basis.

Contact

URL: http://www.hownovel.com
E-mail: intern@hownovel.com

CBS News

General Information: Television News segment of CBS, featuring anchors such as Dan Rather with the Evening News.

Internships Available: News Production Intern. Duties include logging tapes, archive research, time coding scripts, and various other computer and video related duties.

Benefits
Unpaid internship for college credit only.

Contact
Eldra Rodriguez-Gillman
CBS News
524 West 57th Street
New York, NY 10019

Phone: 212-975-5567
Fax: 212-975-8798
E-mail: eig@CBSNEWS.com
URL: http://www.CBSNews.com

Center for Photography at Woodstock

General Information
Not-for-profit arts organization with a goal to promote excellence in photography and the related arts through exhibition, publication, and education.

Internships Available
Photography—responsibilities include assisting in Woodstock Photography Workshop program, summer and fall workshops that involves nationally recognized artist.

Benefits
Non-paid position. Interns can receive college credit. Use of darkrooms and $3000 tuition remission for photography workshop internships.

Contact
Kathleen Kenyon
Associate Director
Center for Photography at Woodstock
59 Tinker Street
Woodstock, New York 12498

Fax: 914-679-6337
URL: http://users.aol.com/epwphoto

Center on Policy Attitudes of Washington, DC

General Information

Center on Policy Attitudes (COPA) is an independent nonprofit organization of social science researchers dedicated to increasing understanding of public and elite attitudes shaping contemporary public policy.

Internships Available

Website Intern—PIPA is in the process of creating a website and needs assistance in the design of the website and web maintenance. Interest in international relations, politics, and public opinion a plus. Internships are available on a part-time basis during the academic year, and full-time during the summer. Application deadline for summer internships is April 15.

Benefits

Paid internship

Contact:
Liz Detter
COPA
1779 Massachusetts Ave. NW
Suite 510
Washington, DC 20036

Phone: 202-232-7500
Fax: 202-232-1159
E-mail: pipa@his.com
URL: http://www.policyattitudes.org

Central Intelligence Agency

General Information

The CIA summer internship program provides undergraduates, particularly minorities and people with disabilities, the opportunity to gain practical summer work experience to compliment their academic studies.

Internships Available

The Undergraduate Student Trainee (Co-op) Program provides undergraduate students with the opportunity to gain work experience on an alternating semester or quarter basis. Students typically spend a minimum of three semesters or four quarters on the job prior to graduation.

The Graduate Studies Program is available for students entering the first or second year of graduate studies. Eligibility is based on a commitment to attend graduate school on a full-time basis following the internship. Most graduate students intern in the summer, however, fall and spring internships are an option. The Graduate student starting salary is around $30,000 per year. Application deadline is November 1.

The Undergraduate Scholar Program is a four year scholarship for high school seniors. The program assists primarily minority and disabled students with demonstrated financial need. Selected students receive a yearly salary and up to $15,000 per school year for tuition fees, books and supplies. Students work summers at an Agency facility and are required to continue employment with the CIA after college graduation. Students must be 18 years of age by April 1 of senior year, with a minimum 2.75 G.P.A. and 1000 SAT score. Application deadline is November 1.

Salaries are paid according to the percentage of course work completed toward the degree. As the student completes additional course work, pay is adjusted accordingly.

Other benefits include: Travel expenses are paid to and from school for non-local students; students receive the same benefits as permanent full-time employees; vacation and sick day accrual; enrollment in health and life insurance plans.

Benefits

Undergraduate student starting salary is typically in the $19,000-$21,000 per year range. The best time to apply is in the Fall of the sophomore year.

Contact
CIA
Recruitment Center
PO Box 12727, Dept. Internet
Arlington, VA 22209-8727

CFN-13

General Information

Affiliated with the Tribune a media company involved in television and radio broadcasting, publishing, education and interactive ventures.

Internship Available

CFN-13 has internship opportunities in the News department. Must attend 16 hours per week per college term.

Benefits

Internships are non-paid.

Contact
CFN-13
Executive Producer
Central Florida News 13
64 E Concord Street,
Orlando, FL 32801

Chevron Corporation

General Information

Chevron Corporation headquarters in San Francisco's Financial District, has openings for interns in the Media Relations group of their Public Affairs Department.

Internship Available

Media Relations Intern—primary responsibility is to produce a daily report of industry news and trends for company management. Scan national wire services, newspapers, magazines and transcripts; select and edit appropriate articles; review with supervisors; and handle layout of the final report. Additional responsibilities include coordinating media training seminars for employees, and researching and monitoring print and broadcast news. Chevron encourages applications from recent graduates or current part-time students in communications, journalism or public relations. Desired skills include: Interest in/understanding of news and current events; knowledge of video equipment; PC proficiency (Word, Excel, E-mail, etc.); news gathering, editing and writing abilities; knowledge of page layout; Internet research experience.

Benefits

Pay starts at $11 per hour, and internships typically last six months or more. Interns qualify for worker's compensation but do not receive health-care coverage or paid holidays.

Contact

Dawn Soper
Chevron Corporation
575 Market St.
San Francisco, CA 94105-2856

E-mail: sopd@chevron.com. (no attachments will be accepted)
No phone calls, please.

Fax: 415-894-8114
URL: http://www.chevron.com

3D Artist

www.3dartist.com

An **ALL** *how-to* print magazine or only $19/year (5 US issues) covering 3D graphics from Poser to Softimage including LW•Max•Maya since 1991!

Visit The Mitch Butler Co.
www.mitchbutler.com
"Chancy" cover image by Mitch Butler
©Copyright 1999 Columbine, Inc.

3D Artist

You can subscribe & take your *subscriber benefits* using the handy **form** at
www.3dartist.com/3dasubs.htm

MAGAZINE SUBSCRIPTION FORM

P.O. Box 4787 • Santa Fe, NM 87502-4787 • USA • 505/424-8945 • fax 424-8946 • orders@3dartist.com

Name _____ Title _____
Company _____ Include apartment or suite #
Address _____
City _____ State/Prov. _____
Zip _____ Country _____
Phone _____ Fax _____
E-mail _____

5 issues for as little as **$19!** Delivered right to your mailbox.

The best hands-on magazine I have ever read. – subscriber

FIVE-issue subscription (about one year) ☐ **NEW** ☐ Renewal
☐ $19 **USA** bulk mail ☐ $25 **USA** 1st class ☐ $26 **Canada/Mexico** Airmail
☐ $31 **West. Hemisphere** Airmail ☐ $35 **Europe** Airmail
☐ $38 **Asia/Africa/Pacific Rim** ☐ $26 surface mail outside North America
☐ **Check/money order** *enclosed* in U.S. funds (no cash or Euro checks)
☐ purchase order attached #_____ (North America Only)
☐ **Visa/MC/AmEx#**_____ Exp. _____

PRINT & sign name

THE FINE PRINT – Satisfaction guaranteed *or money back* on remaining issues. Publication dates vary with 10 to 15 weeks between issues. NOT RESPONSIBLE for issues lost if address change is not given 6-8 weeks in advance. YOUR FIRST ISSUE will be the *current*

Chicago Peace Museum

General Information

The Peace Museum is an educational institution whose mission is to motivate children, teens and adults to achieve creative solutions to the problem of violence. The Chicago Peace Museum is the only museum with a focus on peace in the U.S.

Internships Available

Research, design, photography, exhibition helpers. Skills: Writing, carpentry, database design, editing, fund-raising, graphic design, illustration, public relations, special events planning, typing.

Benefits

Unpaid internship.

Contact

Leah Oates, Exhibition Coordinator
Chicago Peace Museum
314 West Institute Place
Chicago, Illinois, 60610

Phone: 312-440-1860
Fax: 312-440-1267
E-mail: leaho@mail.peacemuseum.org
URL: http://www.peacemuseum.org

Children's Television Workshop

General Information

CTW and Sesame Street were created as an "experiment" in 1968, and the show debuted on November 10, 1969. Designed to use the medium of television to reach and teach preschoolers skills that provide a successful transition from home to school. The show includes learning the alphabet, numbers, and pro-social skills.

Internships Available

Interns may be involved in various aspects production, research, publishing, new show projects, and community education.

Benefits

Unpaid internship for college credit only.

Contact
Children's Television Workshop
Human Resources Department
One Lincoln Plaza
New York, NY 10023

Phone: 212-595-3456
Fax: 212-875-6088

CinePartners Entertainment

General Information

In 1996, CinePartners Entertainment, Inc. was founded for management of the process of feature films and television programs from inception to final product. CinePartners operates in three main areas: creative/production, sales/marketing, and finance.

Internships Available

The responsibilities include: research on the Internet, reading of scripts, evaluation of projects, creation of reader's reports, and following of works in progress. In addition, answering of phones, word processing, filing and assisting the Chairman with works in development. The candidate should have a professional and friendly demeanor, an articulate phone manner, should possess computer skills, and a high degree of organizational and clerical skills. Also a desire to learn about script writing, development, and producing in the independent film community. Non-paid interns whose primary interest is computer graphics, storyboards, movie posters, and design, who have access to a computer and can work at home. Some webpage design knowledge preferred.

Benefits

CinePartners Entertainment has non-paid internship positions available.

Contact
CinePartners Entertainment
10801 National Blvd. #103
Los Angeles, CA 90064

Phone: 310-475-8870
Fax: 310-475-0890
E-mail: cinepartners@jps.net
URL: http://www.cinepartners.net

CLTV News, Chicago, Illinois

General Information

Partners of Tribune Company, a media company with operations in television and radio broadcasting, publishing, education and interactive ventures.

Internship Available

CLTV has internships in the following areas: Editorial, Technical. Production, Sports, Weather, and Marketing.

Benefits:

The CLTV internship program is a hands-on, educational opportunity designed to give students an introduction to the basic skills needed in a news department. All internships are located at up-dated studios in west suburban Oak Brook, IL. This is a non-paid internship.

Contact
CLTV News
Human Resources
2000 York Road, Suite 114
Oak Brook, IL 60523

Fax: 630-571-0489

CNET, Inc. The Computer Network

General Information

Internet resource site, technical information, web-based products and on-line action public company.

Internships Available

Full-time Production Assistant Intern, CNET Software Download. Assist with the production and maintenance of the Mac side of Download.com, CNET's software downloading site. The Production Assistant Intern is responsible for helping to maintain the software library by evaluating titles, entering program specs and writing descriptions, and keeping download links current and functional. Strong interest in and familiarity with shareware and freeware Initiative to take ownership over a project and meet deadlines Excellent communication skills. A sharp eye for detail. Candidates also should be proficient on the Mac platform and have good on-line research skills. Involvement in industry newsgroups, familiarity with Internet protocols and procedures (FTP, Telnet, and so on), and knowledge of HTML are pluses. *Production Assistant Intern, CNET Software download.* Assist with the production and maintenance of the PC side of Download.com, CNET's software downloading site. The Production Assistant Intern is responsible for helping to maintain the software library by evaluating titles, entering program specs and writing descriptions, and keeping download links current and functional.

Benefits

Both high school and college students are eligible to apply; contact school counselors or instructors for possible course credit opportunities. Interns are required to attend training sessions and periodic meetings at the San Francisco office.

Contact

E-mail: kerryp@cnet.com use the words "Production Assistant Intern" in the subject line.

CNN TalkBack Live

General Information

The interns learn the internal workings of a news talk show and how a one-hour show is produced Monday - Friday. Typically, the Audience Coordinators have the most work for interns and manage various responsibilities. The interns help coordinate various marketing and public relations campaigns and are responsible and encouraged to use creativity for advertising TalkBack Live.

Internships Available

Interns have various responsibilities throughout the day. From 2-4 every afternoon the interns work on the set of TalkBack Live. Interns play a big part in the set production; from seating guests, to overseeing the audience warm up, helping with technology to writing name tags and making sure production guests are comfortable. This is a demanding environment and because the show is live, there are very definite deadlines. This internship requires high involvement and serious dedication.

Benefits:

All interns have access to the global Time Warner and CNN internal only job postings as well as a great opportunity to make contacts for future employment possibilities. The internship is a non - paid position, class credits for students.

Contact

Barbara O'Boyle
Assistant Audience Coordinator
TalkBack Live
CNN Center in Atlanta, Georgia

Phone: 404-827-3527
E-mail: barbara.O'boyle@turner.com

College Grad Job Hunter, Inc.

General Information

College Grad Job Hunter, is a Web site for college student and recent graduate job search, has an internship to upgrade the company's Web site graphics. The purpose of the internship is to develop a consistent set of Web site graphics to upgrade the look of the site per current Internet graphic standards, while providing the Intern with experience.

Internships Available

Review the company's current graphics portfolio and make recommendations as to the project scope and schedule for delivery. The Internship will commence immediately upon acceptance of the qualified candidate to complete the Internship and will proceed for the length of time as estimated to complete. This Internship can be completed outside of normal work hours (as a second job or evening job) as long as the scheduled completion deadline is met. Applicants must be current college students and must be willing to commit the time and effort necessary to complete this project within a defined completion schedule.

This Internship will be conducted under a virtual office relationship (i.e., work from a remote location and choose the hours and days to complete the project). The applicant is expected to provide the work space and equipment necessary for completing the work. Daily access to the company's staff is available for both daily and weekly status updates of work progress. An outstanding work ethic and the ability to work independently in meeting a tightly defined schedule is necessary. Highly organized and able to prioritize work to stay highly productive at all times. Self-motivation accomplishes this work independently.

Benefits

This is a paid Internship. This Internship can provide résumé experience to land a paying job after graduation. The successful intern candidate will be selected from among interested respondents based upon necessary experience and time/cost estimate given. Other requirements are experience with a leading graphics program and a portfolio of graphics (Web-based preferred) which are already completed, and ownership of the hardware and software necessary to successfully complete this internship.

If interested, provide the following details via e-mail to the Webmaster: Send a copy of a current résumé as an attached file. The résumé must describe specific graphics experience, including the type(s) of graphics software used in the past. Attach the 5 best examples of graphics development work. In the e-mail, certify that these graphics are owned by the applicant. Provide at least 1 reference (along with contact e-mail address and phone number) of someone who is currently or has in the past used graphics from the applicant. Preference will be given to candidates who have developed graphics for Internet use which are currently being actively used at another site. Provide a narrative (within the body of the e-mail) as to what style and/or formatting to be used for redoing the graphics at the site. Provide samples of work intended. Provide a fixed time (both number of hours and fixed completion date) along with a fixed cost for providing the following specific graphics (hint: provide a short statement of work with a fixed cost and the following graphics as deliverables): Home page header (currently 440x90, but subject to change) Home page map 90x90 graphic representing each of the following locations at the site: Prep; Résumés; Employers; Job Posting; Interviewing; New Job; Search; E-Zine; Forum; Contact; Book; Site logo; 468x60 animated banner advertisement.

Contact
Graphics Development Internship
College Grad Job Hunter, Inc.
1629 Summit Drive, Suite 201
Cedarburg, WI 53012

Phone: 424-376-1000
Fax: 414-376-1030
E-mail: webmaster@collegegrad.com
URL: http://www.collegegrad.com

Columbia Pacific Community Information Center

General Information

CPCIC was created as a means of providing access to computer technology and training for the communities of the Lower Columbia Pacific region. Established in 1996 the center now has 12 employees and have developed a web server which provides information from the Internet to the community at large.

Internship Available

CPCIC has internship for the position of instructor assistant in the computer lab. This individual is responsible for assisting the instructor with classes on the world wide web.

Benefits

This is an unpaid position. Students may receive college credits.
Contact
Link Shadley, Director
Columbia Pacific Community Information Center
1335 Marine Drive
Astoria, Oregon 97103

Phone: 503-325-8502
E-mail: link@ctrf.net
URL: http://www.columbia-pacific.interrain.org

Community Access Television

General Information

Avocacy campaign program

Internships Available

Internships are available through the production department. Interns will assist in producing investigative documentaries and short segments of upcoming events.

Benefits

Non-paid internship. Students can earn college credits through this internship. Students will work as an assistant to producer and director.

Contact
Claudia Pak
Program Director
Community Access Television
307 N. 4th St.
Bismarck, ND 58501

Call Tracy for an application: 701-258-8767

Compulab Inc.

General Information

Compulab is a Miami based web development and networking company that is looking for interns to help out in the process of designing web sites for clients.

Internships Available

The intern will be an integral member of the web development team learning how to develop and prepare graphical interfaces and navigational structures for the web. Knowledge of Photoshop and Illustrator is a must along with some knowledge of the web and HTML. Web Graphic Designer—responsibilities include working closely with a team of designers, and project coordinators to design, develop and implement high-end Internet/Intranet solutions. The job functions entail help with ideas for design theme, creation of graphical interfaces and optimizing of graphics for rapid download on the web. Interns must have knowledge and experience of Photoshop, Illustrator, and some HTML; knowledge of web sites and basic Internet skills, and experience with Microsoft products.

Benefits

Unpaid internship. Students may arrange for college credits.

Contact
Compulab Inc
7340 SW 48 Street, Suite 107
Miami, FL 33155

Phone: 800-962-0659
Phone: 305-669-0707
Fax: 305-669-0806.
E-mail: ivis@compulabinc.com
URL: http://www.compulabinc.com

Cox Interactive Media

General Information
Cox Interactive Media (CIMedia), a subsidiary of Cox Enterprises, Inc. based
in Atlanta, was launched in 1996 to build long-term brands and audiences
on the Internet that would serve local consumers and advertisers in key
markets. Cox Interactive Media has internships in a variety of functions and
locations across the country.

Internship Available
Internships are available in various aspects of New Media.

Benefits
Non paid internships. College credits.

Contact
Cox Interactive Media, Inc.
530 Means Street, NW
Suite 200
Atlanta, GA 30318

Phone: 404-572-1800
Fax: 404-572-1801
URL: http://www.cimedia.com

Creative Time

General Information

Creative Time produces visual arts exhibitions, theater, performing arts and music for the past 13 years, at the foot of the Brooklyn Bridge.

Internship Available

Web Assistant—assist in developing Creative Time's web site which includes authoring new web pages to reflect current and upcoming programming as well as maintaining and expanding the site. Mac experience is preferred, but not required.

Benefits

Unpaid internship, Academic Credit Possible, No Salary, No Housing

Contact

Jennifer Charron, Internship Coordinator
Creative Time
307 7th Ave., Suite 1904
New York, NY 10001

Phone: 212-206-6674 ext. 205
E-mail: jenc@creativetime.org
URL: http://www.creativetime.org

CultureFinder.com

General Information

Established in November 1995, Over 2000 cultural organizations are represented, with links to web sites..

Internship Available

Production assistant—this individual will be responsible for assisting the producer with everyday duties, including editing text and graphics for the Internet. Production assistants may also be involved in the programming of HTML coding and on-line publishing.

Benefits

Interns are paid a stipend for the duration of 3 months, in addition to possible college credits.

Contact
CultureFinder.com
Human Resources Dept.
850 Seventh Avenue #703
New York, NY 10019

Fax: 212-765-4277
E-mail: Jobs@culturefinder.com
URL: http://www.culturefinder.com

Curious Pictures

General Information

Curious Pictures is an international design and television production company producing comedy, graphically inspired live-action, special effects, graphics and animation of all types. The staff of directors, designers, artists and animators produces TV commercials, on-air graphics/titles and television programming. The company was founded in early 1993 as a division of Harmony Holdings, Inc.

Internship Available

Internships are available in animation, computer graphics, stop motion and production.

Benefits

Non paid internships.

Contact
2-D animation—Kris Greengrove
Computer Graphics—Boo Wong
Stop Motion, Props, Sets—Hunt Squibb
Production—Susan Holden Squibb
Curious Pictures
440 Lafayette Street
New York, NY 10003

URL: http://www.curiouspix.com

David Findlay Jr. Fine Art

General Information

Originally a gallery and art supplies store founded over 125 years ago. A supplier of fine art and art supplies.

Internship Available

Internship available in graphic design.

Benefits

Non-paid internship. College credits.

Contact

David Findlay Jr. Fine Art
41 East 57th Street
Suite 1115
New York, New York 10022-1908

Phone: 212-486-7660
Fax: 212-980-2650
David B. Findlay Jr., Lee W. Findlay, Anne Wayson
E-mail: gallery@findlayart.com
URL: http://www.findlayart.com

Digital Domain

General Information

The Digital Domain Internship Program is to promote knowledge of the digital effects industry, and to help develop the skills necessary to succeed at Digital Domain and in the visual effects industry in general.

Internships Available

Internships are available in Features, Model Shop, Commercials, Finance, 2D, Bidding, 3D, Interactive, Animation, System Administration, Stage, Software, Human Resources, Video Engineering, Operations. All Interns must be currently enrolled in a college or university and must obtain a letter from college stating eligibility to earn credit for the internship, and stating the number of units which will be earned. This letter is to be provided to Recruiting/Human Resources. Interns must be at least 18 years of age. Interns may not intern or work at a competing facility during the term of the internship. Interns may not be supervised by a relative or work in the same department as a family member. Interns must be available to work a minimum of 2 days per week. Work hours are to be limited to a maximum of 20 hours per week during the school period (or 40 hours per week during the summer). The length of the internship should not exceed 6 months (without prior approval). Qualifications: Working knowledge of feature film and/ or commercial production. Basic knowledge of the visual effects process/industry. To be considered for an internship, submit résumé and reel (if applicable) along with a cover letter stating area of interest via e-mail, mail or fax.

Benefits

Unpaid internship, no arrangements or pay for living or travel.

Contact

Digital Domain/Recruiting
Intern Program Coordinator
300 Rose Avenue
Venice, CA 90291

Fax: 310-314-2943
E-mail: digitalhiring@d2.com
URL: http://www.d2.com

Digital Imagination

General Information

A multimedia based company involved in various aspects of producing multimedia environments, including presentation, hosting sites, audio-video production, animation, e-commerce, and web design.

Internships Available

Internships are available in multimedia, Internet, and programming. Desired Requirements: knowledge in at least one of the following (and willingness to learn more): Photoshop 4.0+, Director 5.0+, Java, HTML, Flash, Premiere 4.0+, 3D Studio Max, Delphi 4.0+, Java, C++, ASP, or JSP. Residence in the LA or Ventura County area.

Benefits

Paid internship.

Contact

Internet and New Media
Craig Manning
Digital Imagination
2801 Townsgate Rd., Ste. 101
Westlake Village, CA 91361

Phone: 805-497-7303
Fax: 805-230-9208
E-mail: info@digitalimagination.com
URL: http://www.digitalimagination.com

The Dow Jones Newspaper Fund

General Information

The Dow Jones Newspaper Fund is a foundation that encourages young people to pursue careers in journalism. It runs several programs for high school students, college students and teachers. Programs of particular interest to college journalists prepare them for copy editing, on-line editing, and business reporting. The Dow Jones Newspaper Fund has been training copy editors for decades, and the program has earned a good reputation with newspapers.

Internship Available

Copy editing and on-line editing.

Benefits

Formal training, paid internship, and scholarship money available for interns returning to school.

Contact

DJNF
The Dow Jones Newspaper Fund, Inc.
PO Box 300
Princeton, NJ 08543-0300

E-mail: Linda Waller, deputy director

DreamWorks

General Information

DreamWorks Internship Program is a diversity-focused program. The goal of the program is to provide meaningful work assignments to students while building a pool of potential applicants for DreamWorks and the entertainment industry.

Internships Available

DreamWorks Academic Internship Program gives students an opportunity to gain hands-on experience in one DreamWorks department. At the completion of the assignment, the intern should have an understanding of the department function and exposure to the day-to-day operations of the department. This internship may last for the academic semester. Interns participating in the Academic Internship Program must meet the following requirements: Enrolled full-time in an accredited college or university; have an academic major related to the department of interest; able to work a minimum of 12-25 hours per week; able to obtain course credit for the internship.

Benefits

DreamWorks Summer Internship Program Summer Internships give students experience within a specified department over a three month period. Interns are hired on a full-time basis, paid an hourly wage of $6.25 and participate in either special projects or the day-to-day operations of the department. Through weekly Executive Luncheon Seminars, interns learn about various areas of the entertainment business.

Contact

DreamWorks Internship Program
100 Universal City Plaza, Bldg. 10
Universal City, CA 91608

Fax: 818-733-6155
URL: http://www.dreamworks.com

EarthSave International

General Information

EarthSave has a mission to educate, inspire and empower people to shift toward a diet centered around fruits, vegetables, grains and legumes - food choices that are healthy for people and the planet. The primary goal of EarthSave International is to educate the public about the health and environmental benefits of shifting towards a plant-based diet. This is accomplished through educational outreach at both the national level and through local chapters working around the country. Additional goals include providing research to support the educational materials, creating national marketing and public relations programs, building membership and local chapters, and forming alliances with companies and organizations with compatible goals.

Internships Available

Graphic Designer—intern to assist the staff with the creation of consistent graphic templates for local chapter use, including help to design newsletters, special event promotional fliers and posters, display booth signs and materials, and a special need for the redesign of the local chapter operations manual. Web page design, graphic design, illustration.

Benefits

Unpaid internships.

Contact

Linda Amatuzzo
EarthSave International
600 Distillery Commons Suite 200
Louisville, Kentucky 40206

Phone: 206-524-9903
E-mail: EarthSave@aol.com
URL: http://www.earthsave.org

Easynett.com, Inc.

General Information
Easynett is a web presence provider and the Creator of (ALLNY), a comprehensive site on the Internet for everything about NYC.

Internships Available
Varies, typical internships include: *Junior Web Master*—leading to Senior Web Master Position Web Site Administrator and Web Page Designer - CGI and PERL helpful. Basic skills required: Must have basic LINUX and/or UNIX knowledge, Web site Administration knowledge, FTP, Directory tree structure knowledge, etc., some CGI and/or PERL is helpful. Must be highly motivated, mature and responsible.

Web Site Administrator and Web Page Designer—HTML - Web Page Design and Programming must have solid knowledge of the Internet, DOS and Windows. UNIX is very helpful, Netscape Browser Installation and Set-up. Must have basic LINUX and/or UNIX knowledge, Web site Administration knowledge, FTP, Directory tree structure knowledge, some CGI and/or PERL is helpful. Must be Highly Motivated, Mature and Responsible.

Copywriter, Public Relations and Marketing Specialist —excellent written, communication and verbal skills, the ability to self direct and edit copy. Work on projects that are directed to segmented and mass markets. Learn marketing and public relations from the ground up. Work with a team and individually depending on the specific projects. A serious position for people who want to learn and be involved in high-profile serious marketing and PR projects. Exposure to all qualitative and quantitative aspects and the opportunity to contribute creative input in all projects.

Benefits
Very flexible working hours and working locations. This position can lead to possible future employment as well as specific projects that are contracted as

an independent paid contractor. Stock options and bonus programs are available.

Contact
Daniel J. Cohen, Ph.D.
Easynett.com, Inc.
431 5th Avenue 2nd Floor
New York, NY 10016.

Fax: 212-686-9393
All Résumés Should Be Faxed To This Telephone Number Only.

E-mail: ez2000@erols.com
URL: http://www.easynett.com.

EHQ, Inc.

General Information
EHQ, Inc. is a multimedia company based in Hollywood. Among other CD-ROM projects, the company produces high-profile educational series to be released internationally.

Internships Available
Production Administration Intern will assist Production and Creative Team in various aspects of multimedia production in an upcoming project. For those interested in international multimedia, this is an opportunity to be involved in that production process. Knowledge of issues and/or systems of Korea or Asia preferred. Bilingual or past courses in Asian languages a major plus.

Benefits
This is an unpaid internship located in Hollywood, CA. Stipends are to be determined, and receipt of college credits. E-mail or fax résumés and a letter of interest.

Contact
Susana Tsang
Associate Producer
EHQ, Inc.
6777 Hollywood Blvd.
501 Hollywood, CA 90028

E-mail: anasu@ehq.com

Environmental Fund for Arizona

General Information

The Environmental Fund for Arizona (EFA) is a United Way-type organization
that raises money for its member organizations through workplace giving
campaigns. The Graphic Artist/Web Page Design intern assists the director
with development of promotional materials, including one or more of the
following: brochures, posters, web page. Minimum one semester or June-
August commitment.

Internships Available

Graphic Artist and/or Web Page Design Intern. Skills: must submit samples
of work; knowledge/experience in one or more of the following: computer
graphics, illustration, web page design; knowledge of Photoshop, PageMaker
or comparable software; experience designing commercial art. Duties: create
logo, brochures, posters, and/or web page.

Benefits

Unpaid internships.

Contact

Environmental Fund for Arizona
Phone: 602-256-7728
Phoenix or Tucson, Arizona

Experience America

General Information

Experience America is a private cultural exchange organization based in San Francisco, California, dedicated to bringing people from different cultures together through individualized, experiential learning programs.

Internships Available

Vary; personalized for international students and foreign professionals with companies in the San Francisco Bay Area. Placement requires 6-8 weeks.

Benefits

Internships are non-paid and located with companies only in the San Francisco Bay Area. Program fees, terms and conditions can be provided upon request. Interns will receive college credits.

Contact

Rebecca Megerssa,
Executive Director
Experience America
860 B McAllister
San Francisco, CA 94102

Phone: 415-921-3654
Fax: 415-921-3654
E-mail: interns@experienceamerica.com
URL: http://www.experienceamerica.com

Families USA Foundation

General Information

Families USA is the national organization for health care consumers. It is nonprofit and non-partisan and advocates for high-quality health and long-term care for all Americans.

Internships Available

Web Site Intern—gain exposure to current health care issues through updating the Families USA web site. This includes, marking up Families USA reports and other documents, surfing the Internet for various sources of pertinent information, and looking for ways to improve the site. Internet and computer skills are a must; HTML knowledge is desirable. Open to college sophomores, juniors, seniors, graduate students, and recent graduates. To apply, send a cover letter, résumé, and 3 references.

Benefits

Paid internships year-round.

Contact

Internship Coordinator
Families USA Foundation
1334 G Street, NW, Third Floor
Washington, DC 20005,

Phone: 202-628-3030
Fax: 202-347-2417
E-mail: intern@familiesusa.org
URL: http://www.familiesusa.org

Film/Video Arts

General Information

Founded in 1968, Film/Video Arts is a nonprofit media arts center in the New York region. Film/Video Arts provides an environment where emerging and established film, video and multimedia producers of diverse backgrounds can take courses, rent production equipment and edit projects. Film/Video Arts' programs encourage interaction between producers - whether working on narrative features, documentaries, experimental work, shorts, industrials, cable programs, music videos or student projects - by offering services essential to the creation of work and the development of careers. The founders' mission to make the tools and skills of the media arts available to those who might otherwise not have access to them remains the guiding force behind all Film/Video Arts activities and programs.

Internship Available

Film/Video Arts' Internship Program is a six-month program which provides independent film, video and multimedia producers with the opportunity to develop their work by granting them access to Film/Video Arts' courses, production equipment and post production facilities.

Benefits

Individuals accepted into Film/Video Arts' Internship Program are given free access to production equipment and post production facilities when not booked to paying clients. Interns may also enroll in Film/Video Arts' courses at no charge, as space permits. Interns also receive invaluable on-the-job training at a major media arts center. Free access is restricted to use for personal projects and may not be used for freelance work of a commercial nature.

Contact

Internship Program
Film/Video Arts
817 Broadway, 2nd Fl.
New York, NY 10003

Phone: 212-673-9361
E-mail: fva@interport.net
URL: http://www.fva.com

Forests Forever

General Information

Create and locate artwork for use on Forests Forever web site and communications projects. Duties: Produce line art drawings of California nature scenes and species native to California; perform artistic work on projects around the office, such as designing logos or displays; and contact other artists and photographers to locate additional artwork that Forests Forever can use for projects. Qualifications: Excellent artistic skills. Enjoy working independently to generate creative ideas and produce work. Comfortable with taking initiative and being assertive in contacting artists. Commitment to environment.

Internships Available
Art Intern

Benefits
Unpaid internship

Contact
Jolie Dyl
Volunteer Coordinator
Forests Forever
#500 San Francisco, CA 94103

Phone: 415-974-3636
Fax: 415-974-3664
E-mail: jolie@forestsforever.org
URL: http://www.forestsforever.org

Frank Beach and Associates, Inc.

General Information
Founded in 1979 by Frank W. Beach, Frank Beach and Associates, Inc. operates with a core staff of eight professionals. Beach Associates is a communications and media production and consultation business headquartered in Arlington, Virginia, with an extension office in Lexington, Kentucky, and associates located throughout the United States.

Internship Available
Beach Associates offers three different college internships, marketing, video production and new media production. The marketing and new media production interns work under the supervision of the Marketing Manager/

New Media Producer, and the video production intern performs as a production assistant to producers with projects in progress.

Benefits
Internships are unpaid.

Contact
Kay Leonard
Beach Associates
200 North Glebe Road
Suite 720
Arlington, VA 22203-3728

Phone: 703-812-8813
Fax: 703-812-9710
E-mail: kleonard@beachassociates.com
URL: http://www.beachassociates.com/

Free Arts for Abused Children

General Information
Free Arts works with abused and neglected children, and families in crisis in Southern California. Free Arts trains volunteers to work hands-on with victims of abuse. Dance, drama, writing, music, painting and other avenues of creativity are encouraged to channel emotions, release anger and develop positive methods of communication. Artistic expression builds confidence and self-esteem. The philosophy is simple: Art Heals! Free Arts for Abused Children is a 20 year old nonprofit organization that provides creative, enriching and nurturing programs to children who have been abused abandoned or neglected and have been placed in protective custody or the in-patient treatment centers.

Internships Available
Web page design, clerical, fund-raising, graphic design, special events planning. There are 4 programs for volunteers. Children's Special Events — a Saturday, festival of the arts program. 2-3 Saturdays a month-time is 9 am - 2

pm. PACT — an 8-week program geared to help heal families "at risk" using art, music, dance and games that teach communication. Weekly Program - offers continuity to children with a minimum of a 20-week commitment, activities can include arts and crafts, painting, dance, music, photography. The Children's Courthouse Program—Weekday commitment in Monterey Park, CA., offering arts and crafts to families and children while awaiting hearings. There is no charge to volunteers and programs are located throughout Los Angeles, Orange and Ventura Co. Population served: Both sexes: Children, Teens, Adults. Languages: English, Spanish Area of Focus: Arts, Children and Youth, Community Service and Volunteering, Family and Parenting.

Benefits
Unpaid internship.

Contact
Cheryl Silver
Free Arts for Abused Children
11965 Venice Blvd., Suite 402
Los Angeles, California, 90066

Phone: 310-313-4278
Fax: 310-313-5575
E-mail: freearts@earthlink.net
URL: http://www.freearts.org

The Freep

General Information
The Freep is the daily on-line edition of the Detroit Free Press. The Freep offers most of the stories published each day in the printed newspaper, along with added features such as community links, interactive graphics and audio. The Freep updates the stories as they unfold throughout the day.

Internship Available

Detroit Free Press offers 12-week summertime internships in copy editing, design, photography, sports writing, business writing, features and local news reporting and editorial writing. Interns work with professional journalists, taking progressively more ambitious assignments while being supported by editors and professional partners.

Benefits

Interns are paid $498 a week.

Contact

Joe Grimm
Recruiting and Development Editor
Detroit Free Press
600 W. Fort Street
Detroit, MI 48226

E-mail: grimm@freepress.com
URL: http://www.freepress.com

GenneX Healthcare Technologies

General Information

GenneX Health Technologies develops web sites. The company has often been profiled on TV and in magazines.

Internships Available

Web Development Positions: Interns must have a current website. Computer majors with some Java/JavaScript or C, Access, Active Server Page preferred. Design/Art major and experience preferred. Two tracks: 1) art/interface 2) web-to-database/programming focus. Other positions in: marketing, business administration, finance, health writer (women's health). Prefer major and experience related to position sought.

Benefits

Fun, casual atmosphere, paid internships, develop valuable practical skills.

Contact
GenneX Health Technologies
2201 W. Campbell Park Dr. #226
Chicago, IL 60612.

Fax: 312-226-6755.
E-mail: gennex@gennexhealth.com.
URL: http://www.gennexhealth.com

H-Gun Labs

General Information
Two Locations: Chicago and San Francisco the company creates 2-D and 3-D computer animation. H-Gun West (the San Francisco location) produces much of the work in-house. H-Gun West is a MAC/SGI-based facility, utilizing 2-D and 3-D programming.

Internships Available
The internship program at H-Gun West provides individuals with an opportunity to learn all aspects of the production business. Visit and work on the sets of live shoots for music videos, commercials, show openers and show packaging. Involves production assistant duties, from daily runs, set painting and building to craft service, assisting producers, coordinators, and production assistants. Interns observes all aspects of inter-office production, assists all members of the staff in their daily duties: such as dubbing and sending reels; assisting in office communications; answering phones; running errands; creating artwork. During productions, the interns assists production staff with work in the office to assisting with the production and getting a well rounded picture of the production process, from start to finish. Interns with an interest in computer animation and post production editing and special effects will benefit by observing and often participating in the creative process.

Benefits
Unpaid internships. Opportunity for college credits.

Contact
Dawn Smallman or Damon Meena
H-Gun East:
1415 N.Dayton Ave.
Suite 3 South
Chicago, IL 60622
Phone: 312-787-4486
Fax: 312-787-6434
E-mail: info@hgun.com

H-Gun West
587 Shotwell
San Francisco, CA 94110
Phone: 415-648-4386
Fax: 415-920-3911
E-mail: info@hgun.com
URL: http://www.hgun.com

Harvest Moon Community Farm

General Information
Harvest Moon Community Farm assists people in their search for health, meaning, balance, and community in life while nurturing the environment and animals through gardening and agricultural practices, and animal husbandry. The company accomplishes its' mission through the following activities: providing educational materials, and offering informational courses and activities for children, teens, and adults regarding sustainable agriculture and gardening, rural life, nutrition, cooking, wellness, health, animal welfare, and environmental preservation.

Internships Available
Web Page Manager—maintain Harvest Moon's web page through the addition of new information and images, and respond to correspondence.

Benefits
Unpaid internship.

Contact
Ann Rinkenberger
Harvest Moon Community Farm
14363 Oren Road North
Scandia, Minnesota, 55073

Phone: 651-433-4358
Fax: 651-433-4652
E-mail: hmcf@mailcity.com
URL: http://www.geocities.com/RainForest/Canopy/3226/

Historic Films

General Information
Historic Films is an historical stock footage library of moving picture images spanning the 20th century. Over eighty-five individual collections, consisting of approximately 20,000 hours of footage shot between 1897-1985, have been transferred, database, and copyright cleared for production. Over ten thousand vintage music and comedy clips, covering every genre and period of American entertainment, are available, as well as thousands of slice-of-life scenes, TV shows, fads, and musical performances.

Internships Available
Full and part-time internships are offered year-round to college students and other interested parties.

Benefits
Unpaid internships. College credits.

Contact
Historic Films
Kevin Rice, Internship Coordinator
12 Goodfriend Drive
East Hampton, NY 11937

Phone: 516-329-9200
Fax: 516-329-9260
E-mail: info@historicfilms.com
URL: http://www.historicfilms.com

Hodges and Associates

General Information

Hodges and Associates has a 21 year history of architecture. Working with development firms and retailers, Hodges and Associates is licensed in 36 states. Looking for qualified applicants, with CAD experience, to fill the company nationwide.

Internships Available

Intern Architect—Architectural Degree plus 1 year minimum experience. Must be proficient in AutoCAD 14.

Benefits

Paid internship.

Contact

Hodges and Associates
13642 Omega
Dallas, TX 75244

Phone: 972-387-1000
Fax: 972-960-1129

SUBSCRIBE

Industrial Light & Magic

General Information

Founded by George Lucas in 1975, Industrial Light & Magic creates special effects for various blockbuster films including the Star *Wars* series.

Internship Available

The Lucas Digital Ltd. internship program is designed to expose students to various aspects of the entertainment industry. The company offers a variety of positions in such areas as software and information systems, public relations, computer graphics, human resources, web/interactive, editorial, legal, sound, art, feature post production and commercials. Depending on current production projects, they usually hire 10-20 interns each session. The internship application deadlines are as follows: Winter internship applications are due September 13 and Summer internship applications are due by March 1. Applicants who are selected for the program will be notified approximately 2 weeks before the start of the session.

Benefits

The Summer program is full-time and paid minimum wage. College credits.

Contact

Lucas Digital, Ltd. LLC
Internships
P.O. Box 2459
San Rafael, CA 94912

URL: http://www.ilm-jobs.com

Ingalls

General Information

Ingalls is an advertising agency in New England. This is a full service agency, which means Advertising, Interactive Marketing, Design, Direct Response, Public Relations, and Recruitment/Yellow Pages Advertising to clients. All interns will also participate in an intern project working with a team of approximately 6 interns to come up with a branding and marketing strategy for a potential new business prospect. Each intern group pitchs the campaign to senior management and supervisors at the end of the semester. The Ingalls Internship Program is not a rotating program. Interns stay within one department and are supervised by one or two Supervisors. If an intern wants to get exposure to other areas of the Agency, it is possible to set up 3-5 informational interviews during internship. 150 professionals to provide knowledge to student interns. The work flow is set up so one-half of an intern's work will be "project work" and one-half will be administrative. The program is modeled this way so interns experience a typical entry level position.

Internships Available

Internships are offered in the following new media areas: Interactive, Media, Design, Project Management, Creative Services, and Public Relations.

Benefits

Although not a guarantee, many interns have been employed by Ingalls after the internships were completed. Training program specifically designed for interns. Seminars include: Orientation with Ingalls CEO, Direct Marketing, Résumé Writing/Interview Skills, Creative, Strategic Planning, Production , Interactive. All internships are unpaid and require the student to receive college credit.

Contact
Sarah Tillson /Attention Internships
Ingalls
One Design Center Place
Boston, MA 02210

Fax: 617-295-7514

International Cartoons & Animation Center, Inc.

General Information

The International Cartoons & Animation Center, Inc. (ICAC) offers internship positions to gain hands-on animation production experience in the studio. For those new to the field, learn about the complex animation process: the necessary teamwork, dedication, and initiative it takes to solve production problems and make a successful animated film. Get trained through working with a professional animation production staff including producer, film director, animators, layout, background artists, computer artists, and character designers. A chance to apply classroom knowledge to production work in studio. Get experience which can be included on a résumé. If the applicant already has a background in animation, improve skills, obtain production credits, and take advantage of networking opportunities. The ICAC internship may lead to entry-level positions at the company. Although the internship positions are unpaid and there is no guarantee of a job offer after completion of the internship, the company looks first to hire from the pool of interns.

Internships Available

Intern positions are available in animation. Formal application procedure that includes submitting a résumé, sample reel and portfolio, and if selected, interview and evaluation for an intern position. Submit materials to the address below.

Benefits

Working hours and duration of the internship are to be mutually agreed upon by the beginning of the internship. Hours are to be tracked through time-cards that must be filled out and signed by the end of each month. Students should talk to academic or career counselors about getting class credit.

Contact
Mike Soo, Recruiter
ICAC Internship Program
International Cartoons Inc.
1823 E. 17th St., Suite 203
Santa Ana, California 92705

Fax: 714-560-0744
E-mail: icacinc@aol.com

Intrepidus Worldwide

General Information

Intrepidus is a privately owned company with offices in Santa Monica, California operating through two separate groups: broad based media production and entertainment management.

Internships Available

Intrepidus' internship program is designed to give students experience working and learning during each 12 week session. Applicants in: Business Administration, Law, Communications, Computer Science, Accounting, History, Library Science, Film, Graphic Design, Museum Studies and other majors can apply. Several internships are available in the area of web design. Depending on current projects, the company usually hires 2-4 interns each session.

Benefits

Students are paid minimum wage after an initial orientation period of two weeks. Students must receive college credit for the internship. Students must be enrolled in classes at an accredited college located within commuting distance of the internship location. No assistance in obtaining housing, transportation, work permits, or visas.

Contact
Intrepidus Worldwide
Human Resources
3000 West Olympic Blvd.
Santa Monica, CA 90404

Fax: 310-315-4806
E-mail: résumés@intrepidus.com
URL: http://www.intrepidus.com

Isle Royale National Park

General Information

This is a state park accessible by boat or plane. It consists of 165 acres in Michigan. It is a living laboratory and United States Biosphere Reserve. The park encompasses a total area of 850 square miles including submerged lands which extends four and a half miles out into Lake Superior. The archipelago is composed of many parallel ridges resulting from ancient lava flows which were tilted and glaciated.

Internship Available

Photography volunteer—intern will work in the dark room to maintain park photos, documentary photographs and assist with other photographic issues.

Benefits

Housing and meals are free. Use of the darkroom. Non-paid internship for college credit.

Contact

Isle Royale National Park
800 East Lakeshore Drive
Houghton, MI 49931

Phone: 906-482-0984
E-mail: ISRO_ParkInfo@nps.gov
URL: http://www.nps.gov/isro

Jews for Jesus

General Information

Computers and Technology, Network of Nonprofit Organizations, Religion.

Internships Available

Internet Volunteer: Volunteers to work on the web. Opportunities include, but are not limited to hosting chat rooms, writing programs, updating and monitoring content, creating graphics, promoting the organization's web sites. Christians of any age from all over the world.

Web Development Internship—the intern program is for Christians who are college students between the ages of 19 and 25 who have at least one year left of college education. Internships last 8-10 weeks. Internships will take place in San Francisco and run from June to August. Interns are provided with housing one block from the international headquarters in San Francisco. Interns receive a stipend. Description: Hands on involvement in content creation and development. Gain experience in the design of web content and graphics, web programming and multimedia. Specific Qualifications: Have working knowledge of the Internet and web design. Be familiar with image editing programs like Adobe.

Multimedia/Video Production Intern—the intern program is for Christians who are college students between the ages of 19 and 25 who have at least one year left of college education. Internships last 8-10 weeks. Internships will take place in San Francisco and run from June to August. Interns are provided with housing one block from the international headquarters in San Francisco. Interns receive a stipend. Learn pre-production (scripting, scheduling, etc.), production (audio recording, shooting, lighting, graphic creation, etc.) and post-production (editing). Hands-on experience that will include one major project. Electronic Communications major, film/broadcast (radio, TV) major or other related area of study. This is a paid internship.

Benefits
Paid internships.

Contact
Stephen Katz
Jews for Jesus
60 Haight St.
San Francisco, CA 94102

Phone: 415-864-2600
Fax: 415-552-8325
E-mail: jfj@jewsforjesus.org
URL: http://www.jewsforjesus.org

The Jim Henson Company

General Information

The Jim Henson Company is looking for individuals who are organized, mature, flexible, and have a great sense of humor. Interns need not to be a puppeteer, a puppet maker, or an arts and crafts buff to be considered for an internship. Internships are primarily an office and production atmosphere located in either the Los Angeles or New York offices. The company welcomes applicants with a special interest in the Company and its projects. Possible duties and activities are: copying and faxing, assisting with special events, answering phones, assembling materials, running errands outside the office, updating rolodexes, observing production, assisting with mail and filing.

Internships Available

Intern positions are available in both the Los Angeles and New York Offices. Los Angeles Location—the Los Angeles office is the corporate headquarters for the entire company and is home to Jim Henson Pictures (feature film division), Jim Henson Television (TV division) and Jim Henson Interactive (on-line and software division). Offer full and part-time positions with flexible hours in the following areas: office of the President, feature production, feature development, children's television development, prime time television development, Jim Henson Interactive. Internship helps gain confidence in an office atmosphere and see how a production office works. Observe different department interactions, and work in a positive environment. Possession of the following skills is desired: pleasant phone manner, familiarity with Microsoft Word for Windows, good writing skills, knowledge of assorted office duties such as faxing, photocopying, filing, running errands, and answering correspondence, high energy level, ability to work with a team of people, ability to pick up things quickly.

When to apply for LA internships: Spring Semester: applications accepted November - January. Summer Semester: applications accepted March - May. Fall Semester: applications accepted July - August. How to apply for LA internships: Interested in doing an internship at The Jim Henson Company - Los Angeles, send a typed cover letter and résumé to the LA address. Once the résumé is reviewed, the applicant will receive a phone call.

New York Location—Work at least two full days a week, and interns must provide an evaluation upon completion of the internship. There are several departments in which internships are available. All departments prefer a knowledge base of the department's specialty. In addition to the general duties listed above, each department has specific requirements: *Pre-production*— copy and issue scripts, to be good with numbers, have the ability to pick up things quickly. *Publishing*—interest in editing and research. *Public Relations*: Maintain and prepare the monthly clippings package. *Archives/Photo Library*—ability to work with a team of people, assist with photo shoot plans, library or archival background preferred. *Jim Henson Foundation*—interest in Development/Fund-raising, assemble press kits, theater background preferred. *Licensing*—interest in business and marketing knowledge is preferred, computer knowledge, assemble marketing kits. *Studio*—high energy, video and audio dubbing, working with storage facilities, assisting in productions or editing. *Finance*—finance/Accounting major preferred, knowledge of Excel. *Design Services*—assisting in the graphic design department. When to apply for NY internships: Spring Semester: Deadline November 30. Summer Semester: Deadline March 30. Fall Semester: Deadline July 30. How to apply for NY internships: If interested in doing an internship at The Jim Henson Company - New York, send a typed cover letter and résumé to the NY address. After reviewing the résumé, the company will follow up with a phone call.

Benefits

All interns MUST receive college credit. Interns are unpaid and receive a $250.00 stipend for the semester. No housing or transportation. No training in puppeteering or puppet making is offered to interns.

Contact

Intern Program - NY.
c/o Internship Coordinator
The Jim Henson Company
117 East 69th Street, New York
New York, 10021.
Fax: 212-570-1147.

Intern Program-LA.
c/o Nicole Chiasson.
The Jim Henson Company
5358 Melrose Avenue
Suite 300W
Hollywood, CA 90038.
Fax: 323-960-8053.

URL: http://www.henson.com.

Jinil Au Chocolat

General Information

A gift basket company which features chocolate with 2 retail locations, a mail order company, and a web page originally built in 1995

Internships Available

Intern will be working one-on-one with the President of the company exploring ways to increase Internet commerce and traffic to the web site. Updating of the company's web page.

Benefits

Salary and stipends are negotiable, and interns will earn college credits.

Contact

David Sessa
President
Jinil Au Chocolat.
414 Central Ave.
Cedarhurst, NY 11151

Phone: 800-645-4645
Fax: 516-295-2608
E-mail: sas95@aol.com
URL: http://www.jinil.com

KBEG Inc.

General Information

The King Biscuit Flower Hour is a nationally syndicated live radio rock show that began in 1973. The original concept behind the show was to make live rock and roll more accessible to the general audience. The King Biscuit Flower Hour created a stage for bands to have the opportunity to play to a massive audience. In 1995 they began releasing remixed, remastered performances on CD, using the technology of the 1990s.

Internships Available

Opportunities are available in the art department of KBEG for a student to have a creative internship. KBEG is a involved in the creative development of album covers, high end design for the insides of the CDs, and web sites. Candidates will learn about working in the entertainment industry in NYC. Candidates must be creative in art and design with Macintosh experience. Individuals should be interested in creating web sites, illustration and should be an art student. More important than a résumé, send a book —a portfolio or even just a few samples of art and/or design, via snail mail, e-mail in jpeg format or a URL.

Benefits

Unpaid internship, students can receive college credits.

Contact

Keith Morris, Art Department
KBEG, Inc.
18 E. 53rd St. 11th Floor
NY, NY 10022.

E-mail: kemo@kbfh.com
URL: http://www.king-biscuit.com

KCPQ

General Information

A television station in Seattle Washington. All positions arc at the KCPQ Seattle studio facility. Minimum 12-week term. All interns must be college students and provide documentation of enrollment from the institution's internship supervisor. Continuing positions are filled on a quarterly basis.

Internships Available

Various positions available in the following areas:

General News Assistant—student is assigned to the Assignment Editor in the newsroom to work a minimum of 20 hours per week (16 hours for weekend positions) on various shifts. This general position is assigned to students interested in news reporting or assignment editing. Students work with the news staff, specifically the assignment desk, answering phones and researching stories and information for viewers. Accompany reporters and/or news photographers on assignment, or assist a news producer with production. Occasionally, takes news feeds and performs other news gathering functions as assigned by the supervisor.

News Producer Assistant—student is assigned to a News Producer to work a minimum of 20 hours per week (16 hours weekend position) on various shifts. The position is assigned to students interested in news production. The student works with a News Producer, performing news productions functions, with a strong emphasis on story research and writing. Some General News Assistant functions (see above) are performed.

Eng. Editing Assistant—student is assigned to a supervisor in the Eng. Video Editing Department to work a minimum of 20 hours per week (16 hours for the weekend position). This position is usually assigned to students showing an interest in developing video editing skills. The student works with the ENG. supervisor and staff. Students are taught techniques and concepts of Electronic News Gathering (ENG.), including packaging of news stories, tape file research and recording and logging news feeds.

Sports Assistant—student is assigned to work with the Sports Department for a minimum of 20 hours per week (16 hours for weekend position). The student must know sports and comprehend the play-by-play action of sports in season during internship. The student works directly with the anchor or producer compiling scores, researching stories and game information; monitoring televised game (logging action) and accompanying reporter and/or photographer in the field.

Public Affairs—student is assigned to work with the Public Affairs Department for a minimum of 20 hours per week. Student researches and writes twice weekly community calendar; assists in the production of locally produced public service announcements; assists in compilation of FCC quarterly report; assists in research and production of weekly public affairs program, "Northwest Focus." Demonstrated journalistic and writing skills essential.

Sales And Marketing Research—student assigned to the Sales/Research Department for a minimum of 30 hours per week, for students with an understanding and interest in marketing, copywriting skills, personal computers and organization. Juniors and Seniors from college level Business and Communications departments preferred. Intern will assist in the research and creation of presentations for KCPQ's Sales, Programming, News and/or Promotions departments; and aid in compiling research on ratings, programming, clients, competing stations and the television market.

Promotion—student will be assigned to the Audience Development Department and will assist the writer/producers, editors, and staff in all aspects of on-air promotion; including: daily logs, writing, producing and editing. The student will also assist all staff in out-of-house promotional events as they occur. Interns gain a basic understanding of audience development. Applicant must demonstrate interest in a career in broadcast television promotion. Juniors and Seniors from Communication and/or English majors preferred.

Graphics Assistant—student is assigned to the Design Director for a minimum of 20 hours per week. Candidates must demonstrate interest in a career in television graphic design. Intern gains knowledge of television print and on-air graphic design. Duties include layout and paste-up, working with Macintosh computers, observing Quantel Paintbox design, developing reference library and filing.

Benefits
KCPQ internships are not paid positions.

Contact
Keith Shipman, Internship Coordinator
KCPQ Television
1813 Westlake Avenue North
Seattle, WA 98109-2706

Phone: 206-674-1313
URL: http://www.kcpq.com

KGTV, San Diego's 10

General Information
A local affiliate of ABC. The station received its first license in 1926 as KFWV a radio station. In 1953 the station went on air as a television studio.

Internships Available
Internships are available through The Creative Services Department at KGTV/ San Diego's 10. Internships can include projects such as: 1. Learn how to write and produce on-air promotions or public service announcements (for 10 News Close-Ups, Oprah, etc..); 2. Write and distribute a press release or one-sheet; 3. Concept and create a print campaign for a 10 News Close-up.

Weekly Projects—on a weekly basis, interns do one or more of the following: 1. Print and distribute weekly program schedule; 2. Mail and distribute press releases and one-sheets; 3. Write daily voice-over promotions for on-air use; 4. Assist staff members on various projects as needed.

Ongoing Projects—one day a week interns are required to: 1. Answer viewer phone calls; 2. Maintain files for syndicated, local and network programs, including photos, press kits and talent biographies; 3. Other special projects.

Benefits
Unpaid internships.

Contact
Sofia Salgado or
Wendy Urushima-Simmons
KGTV
4600 Air Way
San Diego, CA 92102

Phone: 619-237-1010
URL: http://www.kgtv.com

KPAX TV (CBS), Missoula, Montana

General Information

Television news source in Missoula, Montana with an open internship program. In a smaller situation, KPAX has the ability to offer opportunities unavailable at larger stations or at a network. However there is a limited capacity for interns and therefore a competitive process.

Internships Available

Various positions are offered in television production and related areas including News, Sports, Weather and Producing.

Benefits

Non-paid internship. College credits.

Contact

Paul Shoemaker
News Director
KPAX-TV
2204 Regent
Missoula, MT 59801

Phone: 406-542-4400
E-mail: news@kpax.com
URL: http://www.kpax.com

KQED TV

General Information
Non-profit public access television station.

Internships Available
KQED TV9 has TV Web Internships. Applicants may be undergraduate, graduate or continuing education students with a professional interest in interactive communications. *Web Internship*—tasks include Web research, updating of current content, and development of new content. Interns work with producers on local programs such as Bay Window, the KQED Independent Film Initiative, and other programs in development. Interns work under the direct supervision of the KQED TV program development staff and Web manager. KQED TV seeks highly motivated individuals with excellent oral, written and visual communication skills capable of work independently. Strong multimedia skills, including HTML programming and desktop publishing are essential. Computer science, multimedia production, and graphic design majors are encouraged to apply. Bay Window Production Internship and TV Web Internship are available. 15 to 20 hours per week. Most schedules are flexible. KQED tries to parallel both quarter and semester systems.

Benefits
The internship is non-paid, however, college credit may be available

Contact
Michael Dorame, HR
KQED, Inc.
2601 Mariposa St.
San Francisco, CA 94110-1400

E-mail: hr@kqed.org
Michael Dorame, Human Resources
KQED Job Hotline: 415-553-2209
Fax: 415-553-2183
URL: http://www.kqed.org

KRON-TV Channel 7

General Information

Local NBC affiliates, serving San Francisco Area.

Internships Available

Graphics Department Intern —experience with graphic technology. Duties involve general clerical assistance in addition to researching visual material needed by the department.

News Intern—interns assist assignment editors in various aspects of the news gathering process. Responsibilities include monitoring new sources, answering, screening, and following up on phone calls, updating source lists, and other duties. Interns accompany reporters on stories. Interns work on the news feature "Seven on Your Side," assisting reporters and producers with research for stories, collecting information from various on-line services, maintaining a news database, following up on viewer letters, and assisting with other duties.

Programming Intern—interns assist on the weekly home improvement show, *House Doctor*. Assist in scheduling potential segments, scouting locations, researching segment topics and pre-interviewing guests. Interns work on all aspects of production on all shows.

Benefits

$5 per hour. Internship for college credit.

Contact

Kathryn Cox
KRON TV
900 Front Street
San Francisco, CA 94111

Phone: 415-954-7958
Fax: 415-954-7514
URL: http://www.kron.com

KTLA-TV

General Information
Partners of Tribune Company, a media company with operations in television and radio broadcasting, publishing, education and interactive ventures.

Internship Available
KTLA has internship opportunities in the following departments: News, Graphics, Creative Services, Sales/Marketing, Sports, Community Affairs, Legal, Production, Human Resources.

Benefits
Must receive academic credit for participation (internships are non-paid). Must attend 16 hours per week.

Contact
KTLA Television
Internship Program
5800 Sunset Blvd.
Los Angeles, CA 90028

Phone: 323-460-5527
E-mail: Ktla-hr@tribune.com

KVUE TV (ABC)

General Information
A television station in Austin, Texas. An division of the American Broadcast Companies, Inc.

Internships Available
For the summer session: In production, photojournalism and studio production. *Producer interns*—work with newscast producers and assist the news staff in research, writing, production of newscasts and news briefs.

Photojournalism interns—work with photojournalists and editors to complete assigned video projects.

Studio Production internship—includes working on the studio floor, control room and remote productions.

Benefits

Non-paid internship.

Contact

Sylvia Sedillo, Newsroom Administrator
KVUE TV
P.O. Box 9927
3201 Steck Avenue
Austin, TX 78757

Phone: 512-459-2064
E-mail: sedillo@kvue.com
URL: http://www.kvue.com

KWGN-TV WB2

General Information

Established over 40 years ago, Denver's WB2 was the first station in Colorado and the first with color. WB Affiliate station located in the Denver Tech Center. Partners of Tribune Company, a media company with operations in television and radio broadcasting, publishing, education and interactive ventures.

Internship Available

KWGN Television's internship program offers a diversified experience in a variety of fields enabling the student to learn the expectations of today's employers. KWGN has internships in the following departments: Creative Services/Art, Production, Sales/Marketing, Finance, Programming, Sports, News, Traffic.

Benefits

It is a hands-on educational opportunity designed to give qualified students valuable experience and on-the-job training. Non-paid internships.

Contact
KWGN-TV
Human Resources
6160 S. Wabash Way
Englewood, CO 80111

Phone: 303-740-2222
URL: http://www.wb2.com

Landor Associates

General Information
Landor Associates is an international image management consultancy with 49 years in the design business and offices in 14 countries with over 500 employees worldwide. Specializing in corporate identity, environmental and packaging design. Project teams are interdisciplinary, made up of designers, architects, production specialists, marketing professionals, naming experts and market research professionals. The company creates visual identity systems.

Internships Available
Acceptance is based on a résumé review for all interns, plus a portfolio review for design interns; candidates should have intermediate skills in Adobe Illustrator and beginning skills in Quark and Photoshop. Responsibilities: The design intern participates as a member of a project team on corporate identity and brand/packaging design projects. Design interns create prototypes, assist in preparing for presentations, develop design concepts, assist in production and participate in design critiques.

Benefits
Interns are paid $9.00 per hour. Transportation, room and board and any work permits are the responsibility of the intern.

Contact
Landor Associates
Human Resources Coordinator
1001 Front Street
San Francisco, CA 94111

Phone: 415-365-1700
Contact: Human Resources Manager
URL: http://www.landor.com
E-mail: more_info@landor.com

LAUNCH Media

General Information
LAUNCH Media produces LAUNCH CD-ROM Magazine as well as http://www.LAUNCH.com and other projects as a resource for discovering new music and entertainment through multimedia.

Internships Available
LAUNCH Media Incorporated of Santa Monica is offering qualified applicants an intern position as Multimedia Audio Assistant/Intern. Interested applicants must be familiar with both audio pre and post-production processes including digital recording and editing on PC and Macintosh platforms as well as studio etiquette.

Benefits
Unpaid internship.

Contact
Von D. Burner
LAUNCH Media, Inc.
2700 Pennsylvania Avenue
Santa Monica, CA 90404

Phone: 310-526-4300
Fax: 310-526-4400
E-mail: VonD@LAUNCH.com
URL: http://www.launch.com

Life Online Network, Inc.

General Information

Located at Boston, MA, Life Online Network, Inc., is a portal site (www.lifeonnet.com) and a global service provider in the fields of Internet Services including ISP/hosting, Design, Marketing, Advertising. Also a source of computer hardware, software, electronics, books, music, movies, household appliances and gift services. Partners with the Internet Community like Excite, Microsoft Network and Amazon.com etc. Life Online Network also provides a host of business opportunities through indexing of the revenue generating affiliate programs, network marketing schemes and reseller programs.

Internships Available

Selected Applicants will be working with top management and lead developers in design and development of online malls and scripting software. Applicants must have thorough knowledge of HTML programming and a general idea of web interface development. A knowledge of CGI scripting is a definite plus. Some knowledge of Javascript is also helpful. Freshmen are encouraged to apply.

Benefits

$10/hr but negotiable.

Contact

Debashish D Majumder
Life Online Network, Inc.
50 Island View Place
Suite 309
Boston MA, 02125

Fax: 708-570-1162
E-mail: ddm@lifeonnet.com
URL: http://www.lifeonnet.com

LiveWire Marketing, Inc.

General Information

Web design and marketing company. General resource Internet site.

Internships Available

Production Intern—assistance in production functions which will give an overview of the functional responsibilities of website development and production. Assist in marketing, some client contact, website layout, design, content editing and cleanup HTML markup, minor graphics work, some scripting/coding. Requirements: Must be familiar with HTML, preferably HTML 3.2; familiar with UNIX; familiar with business marketing techniques; familiarity with perl, Javascript, C/C++, cgi experience, Adobe Illustrator, a plus.

Graphics Intern—assistance in a broad range of graphics design; from web-oriented graphics design, layout and cleanup to high quality print design and setup. Functions give an overview of the responsibilities of website graphic design. Requirements: Basic Graphic Design skills and Web familiarity. Knowledge of Adobe/Adobe Illustrator, Macromedia Freehand or Corel Draw7 a must. Familiarity with Macromedia Shockwave/ Director/Flash, DeBabelizer, GifAnimator and 3D experience (Lightwave, 3D StudioMax) a plus.

Benefits

Paid Internship, on-site in Chesterfield, MO $8-$10/hr. Paid or Unpaid internships available.

Contact

LiveWire Marketing, Inc.
Attention: Internship Program
582 Goddard Ave.
Chesterfield, MO 63005

Fax: 314-530-3701
E-mail: internships@lwm.com
URL: http://www.lwn.com

Lovett Productions, Inc.

General Information

Located in the heart of New York's SoHo district, Lovett Productions is a fully equipped production and editing facility. The offices are equipped with Avid Media Composer 400 and 4000's, 3/4" and Beta dubbing machines, and state of the art computer equipment and production office space. The company was founded in 1989 by Joseph F. Lovett, a 10 year veteran and producer at ABC News' 20/20.

Internship Available

Internships are available in the area of production office assistant. The interns work in the area of logging, labeling, videotaping and dubbing videos.

Benefits

Unpaid internships. College credits.

Contact

Rebecca Levi, Office Manager and Internship Coordinator
Lovett Productions, Inc.
155 Sixth Avenue 10th Floor
New York, NY 10013-1507

Phone: 212-242-8999
Fax: 212-242-7347
E-mail: info@lovettproductions.com
URL: http://www.lovettproductions.com

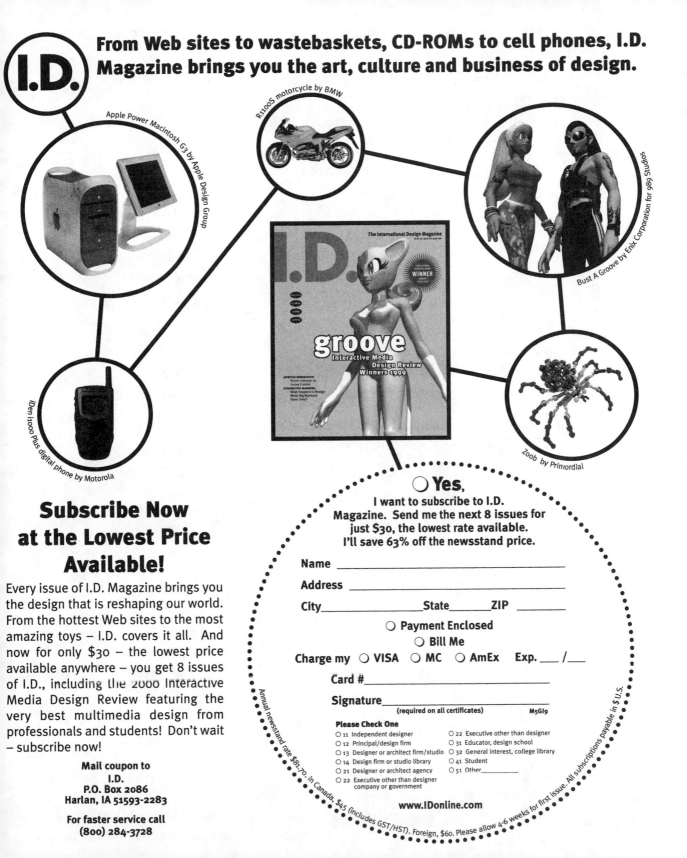

Lucasfilm Ltd. and Lucas Licensing Ltd.

General Information

Based in Marin County, California, Lucasfilm Ltd. is an independent production company, having produced five of the top 20 box office hits of all time and won 17 Academy Awards. The company includes all of the George Lucas' feature film and television activities, and houses the business affairs, finance, information technology and services, research library/archives, Internet, Skywalker Ranch operations, marketing, and human resources divisions.

Internship Available

Assignments may be available in departments such as THX (Pro THX Theaters, Home THX, the Theater Alignment Program and the Digital Mastering Program), Marketing, Finance/Accounting, Human Resources, Information Technology and Services, Ranch Operations (Facilities, Fire/Safety/Security, Organic Garden), Internet, Archives, Library/Research, Business Affairs (Legal), Guest Services, Food Services, and Corporate Fitness. Applications are also available for Lucas Licensing Ltd. which may have opportunities in Domestic Licensing, International Licensing, Merchandising and Publishing departments.

Benefits

Paid internship opportunities in the business aspect of the entertainment industry as well as in various operating departments within the Skywalker Ranch facility.

Contact

Human Resources
Lucasfilm Ltd
P.O. Box 2009
San Rafael, California 94912

Fax: 415-662-2460
URL: http://www.lucasfilm.com

M80 Interactive Marketing

General Information

M80 is an Internet marketing company specializing in music, films, and other new media. M80 Interactive Marketing was launched in the summer of 1998 by former Maverick Recording Company Head of New Media Dave Neupert. Dave's industry experience spans nine years and three major labels (Motown, Capitol and Maverick). M80 uses the street team model that is currently used by most major labels and translates it to the Internet. A grassroots strategy, direct contact of music fans by music fans online, was a strategy that Dave used while working on various projects at Maverick.

Internships Available

Online Promotion Interns—work with bands, films, and other media. Interns market and promote projects online, each project has varying job descriptions. Experience for students interested in entertainment, new media, or the Internet. Interns should have some basic experience with the Internet and should be online savvy. Creativity strongly encouraged. Should be a self starter and motivated.

Benefits

Paid internship. College credit possibilities.

Contact

M80 Interactive Marketing
2301 Hyperion Avenue
Los Angeles, CA 90027

Phone: 323-953-8787
Fax: 323-953-9496
E-mail: neup@m80im.com
URL: http://www.m80im.com

Marco Island Film Festival

General Information

The Marco Island Film Festival is a second year festival with independent and student film competitions in Florida.

Internships Available

Interns to work on the organization's film competitions. The interns would be involved in the many aspects of producing an arts related festival including publicity, operations, finance, scheduling films, arranging seminars and workshops, parties and fund raising. Applicants should currently be involved in a film or arts related program or be considering any aspect of the entertainment field as a career option.

Benefits

Unpaid internship. Opportunity to learn about film and art. White sandy beaches of Marco Island, FL.

Contact

Marco Island Film Festival
P. O. Box 2002
Marco Island, FL 34146

Phone: 941-642-3378
Fax: 941-394-1736
E-mail: info@marcoislandfilmfest.com
URL: http://www.marcoislandfilmfest.com

Marvel Entertainment Group, Inc.

General Information

Marvel Entertainment Group is a comic book company and the creators of Marvel Comics.

Internships Available

Over 30 interns are hired each season. Interns at Marvel assist editors. Responsibilities range from office duties to finding archived images. The duration of the internship is 4 months.

Benefits

Unpaid internship. Interns receive several complimentary comic books each month, T-shirts and super hero buttons. Possible employment.

Contact

Internship Program
Marvel Entertainment Group, Inc.
Human Resources Dept.
387 Park Avenue South
New York, NY 10016

Phone: 212-696-0808
URL: http://www.marvelcomics.com/

McKessonHBOC

General Information

McKessonHBOC is a Fortune 100 corporation and healthcare service company. The company provides a full range of supply management solutions and information technologies. With over 25,000 employees worldwide, the company's primary goal is to improve performance at each point in the healthcare delivery system.

Internships Available

Technical Writer Intern. Must be currently enrolled in college. Position is during the summer only. BS English, Journalism or Technical Writing Internship is in Atlanta, GA. Qualifications: Very strong Word for Windows knowledge, strong Internet experience, good verbal and written communication skills. Description: Perform maintenance on all department files, review all online documents for hyperlinks, format, and consistent presentation, attach latest ISG documentation template to all released documents and compare all online documents to original word file - ensure accuracy. Contact the company for other opportunities.

Benefits
Salary: $10 to $14 per hour; Position Type: Full Time.

Contact
Jeanette Johnson
McKessonHBOC
5995 Windward Parkway
Alpharetta, GA 30005

Fax: 404-338-5122
E-mail: jeanette.johnson@hboc.com
URL: http://www.hboc.com

Media Education Foundation

General Information
MEF is devoted to media research and production of resources to aid educators and others in fostering analytical media literacy, which is essential to a democracy in a diverse and complex society. MEF has produced some 15 videos on issues of media representation and gender, race, violence, and other concerns. It was founded in 1991 by Professor Sut Jhally with the video, *Dreamworlds: Desire, Sex, and Power in Music Video.*

Internships Available
Research and video production. Description: Internships (unpaid) are available to college students, primarily in the 5-college area on Northampton, to assist in the preparation and production of educational videos which analyze the media. Additional internships are sometimes available in research and fund-raising.

Benefits
Unpaid internship.

Contact
Jeremy Smith or Kim Neumann
Media Education Foundation
26 Center Street
Northampton, Massachusetts, 01060

Phone: 800-897-0089 or 413-584-8500
Fax: 800-659-6882 or 413-596-8398
E-mail: mediaed@mediaed.org
URL: http://www.igc.apc.org/mef

Mesmer Animation Labs

General Information
Professional Training for Digital Artists, Authorized Training Center for Softimage, Alias|Wavefront, and NewTek graphics tools. Clients include Microsoft, Electronic Arts, LucasArts, Psygnosis, Boeing, and others.

Internships Available
Internships are open to senior students currently studying at a 4 year college, community college or high school with an emphasis in either the animation, computer graphics, multimedia or art related field. The internship length- 3 months, approximately 3 hours per week. Interns will be required to research a 3D animation related topic and write a 5-10 page paper on the topic, then convert the paper to HTML. Finished research will be published on the Mesmer website. Interns will be required to promote and organize a 3D Animation demonstration at his/her school. Student must submit an application form, a letter of recommendation from an instructor at his/her school, and work of digital art, in either digital or printed form. Internship Applications will ONLY be given out via the Web. Submit 3-4 sentence paragraph on interest in an Internship at Mesmer Animation Labs.

Benefits
Unpaid internship. Students can arrange for college credits. Interns will have the opportunity to take a Mesmer week long introductory course at no cost.

Contact
Matt Ontiveros
Phone: 206-782-8004 or 415-495-1636
E-mail: matt@mesmer.com
URL: http://www.mesmer.com

Minorities in Broadcasting Training Program

General Information
Mission: The Broadcasting Training Program, (formerly the Minorities in Broadcasting Training Program) is a non-profit 501(c)3 organization formed to provide training opportunities to minority college graduates in radio and television news reporting and news management located in Los Angeles, California. The program hosts a monthly online auction with a "Hollywood" theme, has a national membership, a vehicle donation service, and an annual benefit dinner called "The Striving for Excellence Awards." Past keynote speakers have been Dan Rather, Sam Donaldson and Carole Simpson. Supporters include: Montel Williams, Jane Pauley, Connie Chung, Ed Bradley, The Bells of the "Young and Restless" and many others.

Internships Available
TV/Radio News Reporter Trainee; TV/Radio News Management Trainee; TV Reporter Resume' Tape Service—Reporter Resume' Tape Service. Designer of Invitations and Journal—every year there is an annual fund-raiser. The volunteer Graphic Designer will create the invitations and journal for the event.

Benefits
Paid and unpaid internships are available.

Contact
Patrice Williams
Media
Minorities in Broadcasting Training Program
PO Box 39696
Los Angeles, California, 90039

Phone: 818-240-3362
E-mail: office@theBroadcaster.com
URL: http://www.theBroadcaster.com

MJM Family Cancer Services

General Information

Mission: To provide financial assistance and support services directly to cancer patients and their families. Resources are acquired through community oriented fund-raisers and events such as the Mark 4000: Across America Cancer Ride. All events and activities are created and produced solely by MJM Family Cancer Services, a nonprofit corporation of Minnesota. Area of Focus: Family and Parenting, Health, Recreation and Leisure

Internships Available

Computer Development Director. Description: Develop and maintain the corporate web page(s) and ensure a positive presence on the Internet. Design and maintain office database and communication systems. Interns will use software programs such as Microsoft Access, Excel, Word, Powerpoint, Corel 8, WordPerfect 8, HTML to create web page design, database design and graphic design

Benefits

Unpaid internship.

Contact

Mike Juvrud
MJM Family Cancer Services
2309 Wycliff St. Suite 7
St. Paul, Minnesota, 55114

Phone: 651-645-2057
E-mail: mjuvrud@piper.hamline.edu
URL: http://freeweb.digiweb.com/business/mark4000

M&M Creative Services

General Information

M&M is new media design agency. Offers services in Graphic Design, Web Design and Advertising.

Internships Available

Graphic Design Intern—minimum 2 years experience in graphic design, page layout and typography on the Macintosh platform. Working knowledge of 5.0, Pagemaker 6.5, Illustrator 8.0 and MacOS 8.5. Applicant must have developed typography skills and a firm grasp of basic graphic design concepts. Extensive portfolio, knowledge of 4 color printing and real life experience a plus.

Benefits

Unpaid internship. Potential to give the interns valuable hands-on responsibilities.

Contact

M&M Creative Services
Kolin Rankin
P.O. Box 2457
Tallahassee, FL 32316

Phone: 888-224-1169
E-mail: rankink@thinkcreative.com
URL: http://www.mmdg.com

Moline Dispatch Publishing Company

General Information

The Dispatch and The Rock Island Argus are the Illinois Quad-Cities hometown news sources. Distributed throughout Rock Island, Henry and Mercer Counties in Illinois and portions of Scott County, Iowa. Circulation of over 40,000.

Internships Available

Photography—photography intern shoots the news and feature photos for publication in the daily newspaper. Intern function as a staff photographer with a 40-hour work week.

Benefits

$200 per week in addition to college credit.

Contact

Russ Scott
The Rock Island Argus
1724 4th Ave.
Rock Island, IL 61201

Phone: 309-797-0345
URL: http://www.qconline.com

Morningstar, Inc.

General Information

Chicago-based Morningstar provides mutual fund, stock, and variable-insurance investment information. An independent company, Morningstar does not own, operate, or hold any interest in mutual funds, stocks, or insurance products.

Internship Available

Design internships offered in the following disciplines: Editorial/Product, Marketing, and Web/Electronic design. Design Intern—this is an internship opportunity for those interested in web, promotional/advertising and print design. The intern will be involved in various stages of a project ranging from product and marketing strategy, to conceptualization, to design and production. Former interns have produced brochures, magazine and newspaper ads, in-house invitations, posters, and other communication materials. Students can expect to work closely with staff designers, copywriters, product managers, and editors, as well as people in other departments.

Benefits

Possibility for paid internships. College credits.

Contact

Morningstar, Inc.
225 W. Wacker Drive
Chicago, IL 60606 USA

Phone: 312-696-6000
800-735-0700
E-mail: recruit@morningstar.com
URL: http://www.morningstar.com

MonsterSwapper.com

General Information

Internet start-up needs summer interns for nationwide web project. Territory managers and supervisors needed in all states for three month effort. Monsterswapper.com is founded by crack executive team made up of M.I.T. grads, Internet and marketing professionals who have worked for industry giants like IBM, ITT, Stanley Tools, Ameritech, Champion Paper and Nextel.

Internships Available

Open to students with access to a computer, knowledge of Excel, an e-mail account. Requires a minimum commitment of 20 hours per week. Work from home on flex-time.

Benefits

This is an unpaid internship and there are no stipends or college credits awarded. Students gain job experience, promotions, a position title for résumé, and references from industry professionals. Send résumé as e-mail attachment in Word 95 format.

Contact
Mark Anderson
President
MonsterSwapper.com
3 Olde Meetinghouse Rd.
Westborough, MA 01581

Phone: 508-898-9716
E-mail: MarkAnderson1@hotmail.com
URL: http://www.monsterswapper.com

MTV, Music Television

General Information

Cable television station that was founded in 1981, MTV produces cartoon and music related television programs.

Internships Available

Various internships are available. MTV hires over 150 interns each session to work in such areas as business, press and public relations, art promotions, talent relations, graphics, on-air talent, video library. Students may also work on specific MTV programs. Interns work for an average of 3 weeks. Local Stringer—serve as stringer, reporting on music happenings and other grass-roots items of interest to MTV viewers in the area. Requires knowledge of music and pop-culture and strong writing skills.

Benefits

Unpaid internship. Interns attend free live taping of shows. Free luncheons. Interns will receive school credit; opportunity to add to résumé and research skills, and free MTV stuff. Local Stringers receive up to $25.00 maximum weekly allotment covering expenses incurred while on the job.

Contact
MTV
Internship Program
1515 Broadway, 22nd Floor
New, York 11036

MTVRep@MTVmail.com.
URL: http://www.mtv.com

Museum of Contemporary Art

General Information

The Museum of Contemporary Art (MCA) exhibits thought-provoking art created since 1945. Documents contemporary visual culture through painting, sculpture, photography, video and film, and performance. Located in downtown Chicago, the MCA consists of a gift store, bookstore, restaurant, 300-seat theater, and a terraced sculpture garden. The MCA's mission is to collect, preserve, present, and interpret contemporary art and to engage a broad and diverse audience through these activities.

Internship Available

The Museum of Contemporary Art internship program takes place in a professional not-for-profit museum environment. Over 18 departments offer experiential education in a hands-on environment in exchange for a substantive contribution from talented and interested students and graduates.

Through a grant from the Lila Wallace Reader's Digest Fund Museum Collection Accessibility Initiative, interns are incorporated into an Advisory Board to assist with the goals of the grant, cultivate interest in contemporary art among the Chicago college student population, and promote long-term involvement in the arts. The Museum of Contemporary Art seeks increased diversity in its intern staff and provides equal opportunity to its applicants. Internships are available in the following areas:

Graphic Design—design interns work with the Director of Design and Publications to develop and produce materials related to the MCA's graphic needs, including exhibition catalogues, gallery signage, and brochures. Candidates should have experience in print production and Macintosh. Applicants should include slides or samples of work with application. Design course work or graduate or undergraduate degree candidates preferred.

Information Systems—interns assist Director of Information Systems with the overall implementation and supervision of information systems in all museum departments and operations. Duties include routine maintenance of hardware, performing diagnostics on PCs, Macs, and the mainframe.

Multimedia—intern will assist the MCA's designer of Interactive Media with developing new technologies associated with Stir It Up, a program made possible by a grant from the Lila Wallace-Reader's Digest Fund. The program's goal is to reach the large population of computer users in the target audience of 18-24 year-olds. Candidates with strong media/technology background will be considered to assist with the creation and implementation of the MCA's Homepage on the World Wide Web as well as collaborate with staff to develop various interactive kiosks and on-line computers in galleries. Experience with design and the Internet highly preferred. Must have experience with a number of computer programs. By utilizing the PICK/BASIC computer language, interns have the ability to spot and troubleshoot software/hardware problems. Course work in computer sciences or equivalent experience necessary.

Performance Programs—interns assist the Director of Performance Programs in various aspects of developing and producing MCA programs in performance art, dance, music, literary arts and film and video. Interns develop and maintain resource files, prepare for review of artists' proposals, and assist with clerical and administrative tasks. Internship includes assistance with event management related to performance programs. Undergraduate studies in art history or studio arts required, and performing arts background preferred. Computer skills and basic administrative experience necessary.

Photo Archives—interns organize, label, and photograph documentation of the Permanent Collection and temporary exhibitions. Interns facilitate rights and reproduction requests including copyright, correspondence, and invoice tracking. Interns also work with the MCA photographer to process internal work requests, log photographic material and local photo lab requests, and further develop a long-term photo archive program. Experience with photography and/or photo processing is helpful; art background is preferred.

Benefits

Unpaid internships, college credit available, access to job listings, letter of recommendation.

Contact

Museum of Contemporary Art Chicago
220 East Chicago Avenue
Chicago, Illinois 60611

Phone: 312-280-2660
TDD: 312-397-4006
Fax: 312-397-4095
Intern Coordinator: 312-397-3822
E-mail: hconvey@mcachicago.org
URL: http://www.mcachigago.org

NARAL of New York

General Information

NARAL/NY is a political, grassroots membership organization that seeks to guarantee the right to legal, accessible and safe abortion and to support reproductive rights for all women.

Internships Available

Computer Intern—the intern will help build NARAL/NY's web page, improve the computer network, and assist in training staff. Excellent computer skills required. *Graphic Designer*—organization seeks freelance graphic designer for publications, invitations, brochures.

Benefits

Unpaid internship.

Contact
Kim Gerstman
NARAL of New York
462 Broadway, Suite 540
New York, New York, 10013

Phone: 212-343-0114
Fax: 212-343-0119
E-mail: NARALNY@aol.com

The Nautilus Institute for Security and Sustainable Development

General Information

A policy-oriented research organization Asia-Pacific regional security and ecologically sustainable development. Area of Focus: Economic Development, Environment, Peace and Conflict Resolution

Internships Available

World Wide Web Intern—assist with various aspects of World Wide Web site updating. Responsibilities will include: Web page design, editing, graphic design

Benefits
Unpaid internship

Contact
Steve Freedkin
The Nautilus Institute for Security and Sustainable Development
1831 Second St.
Berkeley, California, 94710

Phone: 510-204-9296
Fax: 510-204-9298
E-mail: nautilus@nautilus.org
URL: http://www.nautilus.org

The Naval Historical Center

General Information

Official history program of the Department of the Navy. Its lineage dates back to 1800 with the founding of the Navy Department Library by President John Adams. The Center includes a museum, art gallery, research library, archives, and curator as well as research and writing programs. The mission is to enhance the Navy's effectiveness by preserving, analyzing and interpreting its experience and history for the Navy and the American people, through a series of chronological and thematic exhibits. Currently, the staff is producing exhibits on the Civil War.

Internship Available

Internships are available in four specialties at The Navy Museum. Two of these— historian and education specialist— coincide with college departments. The third, public relations, provides an opportunity for a college student to gain work experience in a field suitable for any liberal arts student. The fourth, with the Design Department allows specialized training for graphics and studio art majors.

Design—the design intern will assist in all phases of mounting major exhibitions and responsibilities may include model-making, preparing shop drawings, typesetting, graphic photography, photo silk-screening and mounting photographs. The intern may also assist in preparing the artifacts for installation.

The intern may also select a project related to the needs of the Museum, the intern's abilities and interests, and the length of the internship. The intern works with the Curator or project director responsible for the exhibition, publication or event, but under the supervision of the head of the Design Department. A graphics project might involve developing a design solution and preparing camera-ready art for a small museum publication or a series of graphic materials for an upcoming exhibition or event. The project might also involve the design of a small installation in the Museum The intern would take this project from concept stage through working drawings to installation.

Benefits
The Naval Historical Center provides no salaries or other stipends to interns. If the center's funds permit, small honoraria may be paid to interns. If available and appropriate, these honoraria will average about $20.00 per day and will be limited to a total of $400 for each intern.

Contact
Dr. Edward Furgol, Curator
The Navy Museum
Naval Historical Center
805 Kidder Breese SE
Washington Navy Yard
Washington, DC 20374-5060

Dr. Furgol, Intern Coordinator
Phone: 202-433-6901
Fax: 202-433-8200
efurgol@nhc.navy.mil

New York Times

General Information
The New York Times Company is a public corporation that publishers of the New York Times, a news national newspaper that covers regional and international news, sports, weather and events. The Paper accounts for 91% of the company's total revenues. Circulation of 1,094,100 on weekdays 1,644,800 on Sundays.

Internships Available
Internship positions available in the following departments: Art Desk, Graphics Desk, and Photography Desk. Additional Paper's Summer Internship Program for Minorities; interns write a total of 12-22 stories. Interns learn copy editing skills, newspaper design and aspects of photojournalism and

attend biweekly seminars featuring reporters, editors, bureau chiefs, correspondents and columnists. 10 weeks program.

Benefits

Paid and Unpaid internship for college credit only.

Contact

New York Times Company
Internship Programs
229 West 43rd Street
New York, NY 10036

Phone: 212-556-4412
URL: http://www.nytco.com

Nickelodeon Animation Studio

General Information

A Viacom International, Inc. company. Nickelodeon Animation Studios produces and creates several cartoon shows.

Internships Available

Production internships available; a letter from the school will be required if chosen as an intern.

Benefits

Unpaid internships. Must be able to receive academic credit for the internship.

Contact

Jill Shinderman
Nickelodeon Animation Studio
231 W. Olive St.
Burbank, CA 91502

Fax: 818-736-3539
E-mail: fairk@mtvn13.viacom.com

The North Carolina State Parks System

General Information

The mission is to conserve and protect representative examples of the natural beauty, ecological features and recreational resources to provide outdoor recreational opportunities in a safe and healthy environment; and to provide environmental education opportunities that promote stewardship of the state's natural heritage.

Internship Available

Photography intern—responsibilities include assisting with park documentary.

Benefits

Free housing, possibilities of receiving college credits. Unpaid internship.

Contact

North Carolina Division of Parks and Recreation
PO Box 27687
Raleigh, NC 27611-7687

Phone: 919-733-4181

NOVA Online

General Information

Launched in 1996, NOVA Online (www.pbs.org/nova) seeks to enhance the content of NOVA programs through text, images and interactive games as well as generate new content in the form of "online adventures."

Internships Available

Internship duties and responsibilities include telephone and library research, stock photo research, converting video and photographic material to digital media, manipulating that media, reading and answering e-mail and generally assisting the personnel in the department. An example of a part-time Summer internship opportunity is in the Online division is the WGBH Science Unit, which produces the PBS science series NOVA.

Benefits

Applicants must be full-time students willing to work 15-20 hours per week. Scheduling is flexible, but students must be receiving academic credit for the internship. This is an unpaid internship, and there are no stipends.

Contact

Jen Uscher
Production Assistant
NOVA Online
125 Western Ave, Boston MA 02134

Phone: 617-492-2777 ext. 4259
Fax: 617-787-7843.
E-mail: Jennifer_Uscher@wgbh.org
URL: http://www.pbs.org/nova.

The Office of Imaging, Printing and Photographic Services

General Information

The Office of Imaging, Printing and Photographic Services is the Smithsonian's central source for the creation, processing, distribution and archival storage of photographs and digital images.

Internship Available

Electronic imaging interns—interns are responsible for assisting with photo CD production, digital restoration, scanning images, researching on-line, cataloging images.

Benefits

Unpaid internship. Possible college credit exchange.

Contact
The Office of Imaging
Printing and Photographic Services
Smithsonian Institution
American History Building, Room CG054
Washington, DC 20560-0644

Contact: Lori Aceto
Phone: 202-786-2707
Fax: 202-357-1853
URL: http://photo3.si.edu

Omni Internet

General Information
Internet team creating an Internet (and only existing) version of a magazine converted to an interactive website position.

Internships Available
Intern will be part of the company's creative team, and should arrive with significant computer skills, especially HTML programming and a journalism background is a plus. This is an online (and only existing) version of a magazine, and publishes a broad range of content covering science and technology, science fiction, net culture and the arts. The internship will focus on web design and production, with some general office work (like sorting through the mail) thrown in as well.

Benefits
This internship pays $500 per month, and there are no stipends. Interns will receive college credits. If interested, send a résumé to the e-mail address.

Contact
Internet Pam Weintraub
Editor/Producer
Omni Internet
E-mail: pam.weintraub@generalmedia.com
URL: http://www.generalmedia.com

Paradesa Media

General Information

The company develops web sites, intranets, extranets and creates multimedia programming for broadcast and cable television, laser disc, CD-ROM and online services. Offers development services for both public and private sites, including: interface and graphic design, information design, website development and maintenance, development of intranet applications and databases. Clients include Bank of America, Genstar Instant Space, Piper Jaffray, Thelen, Marin, Johnson & Bridges, The California Trust, West Coast Industries, Bay Area Multimedia Partnership, and Studio Z.

Internships Available

Graphics and Animation intern—an education in graphic art or animations good technical understanding of graphics software and the World Wide Web. Priority is given to students from Rhode Island School of Design. *Programming intern*—responsibilities include creating software to deliver multimedia content. Programmers must be creative and imaginative in the use of Lingo and Java.

Benefits

Paradesa Media offers unpaid internships in online publishing and website development. Bilingual abilities and translation expertise helpful, but not mandatory.

Contact

Paradesa Media
375 Alabama Street
San Francisco, California 94110

Phone: 415-826-2727
Fax: 415-487-2030.
E-mail: jobs@paradesa.com
URL: http://www.paradesa.com

The Partos Company

General Information
Talent agency for artists, directors and designers of the film and commercial ad industry. The Partos Company was established in 1991.

Internship Available
Internships are available in the area of web design and content creation. Responsibilities include research, graphics design, and writing articles.

Benefits
Paid or unpaid internship.

Contact
The Partos Company
A Talent and Literary Agency
6363 Wilshire Blvd.
Suite 227
Los Angeles, CA 90048

Phone: 323-951-1320
Fax: 323-951-1324
URL: http://www.partos.com

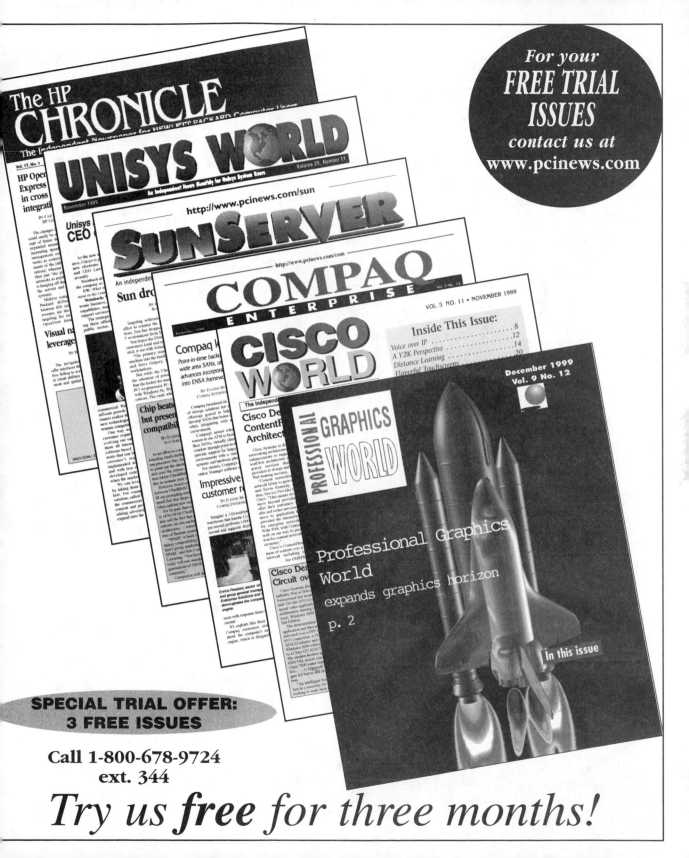

Educate Your Imagination

The future of computer graphics is in the imagination. And your imagination can be stimulated, excited and informed by *Computer Graphics World*. Every issue is filled with mind expanding articles that explore leading-edge tools and techniques in the rapidly evolving world of visual graphics. Whether your interest is in CAD/CAM, film and broadcast, multimedia, interactive entertainment, desktop video, scientific visualization, architectural CAD or web creation, you can count on *Computer Graphics World* for your inspiration and information.

Call now for subscription information!
1-847-559-7500

COMPUTER GRAPHICS WORLD

www.cgw.com

Pixar Animation Studios

General Information

High end animation studio based in Northern California. The company creates three dimensional animation shorts and feature films in a partnership with The Walt Disney Company.

Internships Available

Archive/Creative Resources Intern Division—creative Resources, Pixar Archive Internship Dates: March - August. Responsibilities include archiving: help organize and file all reference and original artwork from feature and short films. Create archival process for pastels and paintings. Building of organizational binders (photocopying and breaking down into categories). Create appropriate shelving for props and sculptures. Facilitate transportation of materials to temporary storage space. Facilitate the establishment of a library system for all reference books and magazines Pixar-wide. Order supplies as needed. Facilitate any Pixar-wide requests for artwork or reference.

Creative Resources—report to Department Manager and Coordinators to assist in the operations of department. Respond to the needs of the Creative Resources group, the Marketing group, and the Disney Consumer Products group; may involve administrative duties in addition to general production assisting or support. General areas of responsibilities include: Data entry. Maintaining the artwork flat files. Work with the CR Department Manager and other department staff to maintain a complete database of all materials requested and sent out. Work with Archivist to designate art for Creative Resources or Archive storage. Copying (standard and color). Printing reports. Note taking and distribution. Systems requests (submitting work orders). Ordering lunches, occasional runner work (film runs, lunch/dinner runs, art supplies). Meeting Preparation. Set up and breakdown of conference rooms/ screenings, etc. Shipping of film, videotape, data tapes, artwork and other production materials. Update art boards displays. Scanning art as needed.

Acting as key link to Archive for storage and tracking of artwork and maintenance of art/reference binders.

Qualifications: Computer (Mac) literacy is essential., Illustrator and UNIX skills are a plus. Ability to interpret abstract artistic direction and to provide clear notes based on fast-paced art review meetings. Familiarity with the artistic process, art materials and supplies preferred. Film production, Art, and/or Marketing background preferred. General office skills. Excellent organizational skills. Attention to detail. Multi-tasking skills. Self-starter. Eager to learn. Problem solver. Highly motivated team player. Friendly and positive attitude. Must have a car, insurance and valid drivers license.

Benefits
Contact the company.

Contact
Pixar Animation Studios
Recruiting
1001 West Cutting Blvd.
Richmond, CA 94804

Jobs Hotline: 510-412-6017
Fax: 510-236-0388.
E-mail: hr@pixar.com.
URL: http://www.pixar.com

Portland Art Museum, Northwest Film Center
General Information
The Portland Art Museum Northwest Film Center is a regional media arts resource and service organization based in Portland, Oregon founded to encourage the study, appreciation and utilization of the moving image arts, foster their artistic and professional excellence, and to help create a climate in which they may flourish. The Center provides a variety of film and video exhibition, education and information programs primarily directed to the residents of Oregon, Washington, Idaho, Montana and Alaska.

Internship Available

Education Intern—the Education Intern will gain a working knowledge of the operations and services of one of the country's largest regional media arts centers. The Intern will also develop organizational, administrative and interpersonal skills which can later be applied in a wide variety of employment situations. Specific technical skills in film and video production will be learned, including operation of projectors, editors, and cameras. Duties and responsibilities: assists the Equipment Manager with equipment checkout, inventory control, and sale of film supplies. Assists in monitoring use of video and film editing facilities, dubbing and transfers. Coordinates special projects associated with education program; general clerical duties associated with above. May also act as class assistant for production classes, duties including classroom set-up, preparing materials for faculty members, and operating film/video projectors.

Qualifications: Basic knowledge of film and video equipment. Digital experience desirable; ability to work effectively with students, faculty, staff, and the general public; must be organized and methodical with a strong attention to detail; must be able to work creatively with limited resources; word processing skills on Macintosh computers desirable; PC experience helpful.

Benefits

Unpaid position. Interns will have free admission to Film Center exhibition programs (excluding special admission and festival programs). Tuition waived for classes and seminars and equipment rental.

Contact

Northwest Film Center
Richmond Communications LLC
1219 SW Park Avenue
Portland, Oregon 97205

Phone: 503-221-1156
Fax: 503-294-0874
E-mail: info@nwfilm.org
URL: http://www.nwfilm.org

The Presidio Trust

General Information
The Presidio Trust, a non-profit Federal Government Corporation, manages and preserves the historic, cultural, and natural resources of the Presidio National Park in San Francisco, a former military base dating back to 1776. A growing community of organizations and businesses that fit park goals make their home at the Presidio, enjoying a full range of workforce housing and the amenities of a national park setting.

Internships Available
Computer Design Intern—candidate should be interested in some or all of the following areas: computer aided design, graphic art, maps, architectural design, and CAD management. Involves producing presentation materials such as maps and brochures and/or working with architectural plans. Applicant must be an undergraduate or graduate in graphic art. Good computer knowledge, a design background, and preferably knowledge of more than one of the following computer programs: AutoCAD R14, AutoCAD Map, Architectural Desktop, Visio, 3D Studio, Illustrator,, and/or PhotoDeluxe. Additional areas of interest could include multimedia, animation, web design, and database programming.

Benefits
Position is through the summer (approximately 10 weeks), and includes salary of $10/hour plus housing on-site at the Presidio.

Contact
Sara Fain
The Presidio Trust
P.O.Box 29052
34 Graham Street
San Francisco, CA 94129

Phone: 415-561-5351
Fax: 415-561-5315
E-mail: sfain@presidiotrust.gov
URL: http://www.presidiotrust.gov

REI Media Group

General Information

REI is involved in a collaborative effort encompassing creative and technical elements. REI Media Group is a film optical house for service to filmmakers. REI Media Group works as a part of a team - rather than an impersonal outside service. REI Media Group creates title design, optical effects, digital effects, blowups, and design services for posters, press kits and advertising services for new filmmakers and companies such as Paramount, 20th Century Fox, Columbia, Sony, New Line, Miramax and Buena Vista.

Internship Available

Film post production and animation effects internships.

Benefits

Unpaid internships. College credits.

Contact

REI Media Group
28 West 39th Street
New York, New York 10018

Phone: 212-768-9300
Fax: 212-768-0438
E-mail: reimedia@aol.com
URL: http://www.reimedia.com

R/GA Digital Studio

General Information

R/GA Digital studios consist of two major departments—R/GA Interactive and R/Greenberg Associates. Established in 1993, R/GA Interactive is a strategic design agency that creates web sites, kiosks, CD ROM and games for companies. With over 20 years experience R/Greenberg Associates is an Academy Award-winning digital production company that creates visual effects, 3D graphics, design and motion graphics.

Internship Available

Animation, multimedia, and various forms of new media internships are offered year round.

Benefits

Possibility for employment after internship. College credits. Non paid internship.

Contact
Peter DeSouza
Human Resources
R/GA Interactive
350 West 39th Street
New York, NY 10018

Phone: 212-946-4060
Fax: 212-946-4010

E-mail: peterd@rga.com
URL: http://www.rga.com

Rhythm and Hues

General Information

Rhythm and Hues is a high-end computer-generated animation production company.

Internships Available

Requirement for an animation internship position at Rhythm and Hues includes submitting a demo reel accompanied by a short explanation of each piece on the reel. In the case of team projects, note the aspects for which the applicant was responsible. A portfolio of artwork will also be accepted for consideration. Slides or copies are fine. For the Summer animation internship program, it is best to submit an application before May. To apply for animation internships during the school year, please send a cover letter, résumé, and demo reel of work, 1/2" VHS or 3/4" U-matic tapes are fine; no Beta, please. NTSC format is preferred. Please no disks, CD-ROMS, or web sites. Describe weekly availability in the cover letter.

Another internship program is for programming interns, and is geared towards graduate students (i.e. people working on Master's Degrees or Ph.D.'s). This internship is also a paid position. Programming graduate students, please submit a résumé and include a cover letter indicating interest in the programming internship.

Internships in the Art/Production Design department are also sometimes available. These internships are usually paid, and tasks may range from art assistance, such as art work clean-up, to actual production design, depending on ability level. To apply, send resume and a copy of portfolio with a cover letter indicating interest in the art department internship.

Benefits

Three-month long, paid positions involving one month of training on proprietary software, followed by assisting a Technical Director on actual production.

Contact

Recruiting
Rhythm and Hues Studios, Inc.
5404 Jandy Place
Los Angeles, CA 90066

Phone: 310-448-7619
Fax: 310-448-7600
E-mail: recruitment@rhythm.com
URL: http://www.rhythm.com

Richmond Communications LLC

General Information

New Internet company launching an e-commerce site.

Internships Available

Interns will be involved in all aspects of the design of an e-commerce site and preparation for launch. Primary responsibilities include design of content, conversion of text and layout.

Benefits

This is an unpaid internship, and there are no stipends.

Contact

R. Hurowitz, President
P.O. Box 1539
New York, NY 10021

Fax: 212-808-4648
E-mail: PuppyHse@aol.com

Robert M. Brandon & Associates

General Information

Robert M. Brandon & Associates is a small public affairs and strategic management firm specializing in organizational development, public interest and grassroots advocacy, and local and international development initiatives.

Internship Available

Public Affairs Intern—Brandon & Associates offers internship opportunities to undergraduate and graduate students interested in working in public affairs with a public interest focus. Learn about how politics and policy making, the media, and grassroots activities intersect. Interns have the opportunity to engage in public affairs activities. Depending on individual interests and skills, interns may: track state and federal regulatory issues affecting consumers; participate in grassroots organizing efforts; research public policy issues; conduct media outreach; design and maintain web sites; maintain press, policy maker and contact lists; and perform general administrative duties as needed. The internships largely are timed to the academic calendar. To apply in a timely fashion, candidates for summer internships must provide materials to Brandon & Associates by April 30, for fall semester internships, by September 15, for spring semester internships; by January 15. Each intern at Brandon & Associates will possess some or all of the following professional attributes: excellent written and verbal communications skills, strong research skills, editing experience, superior organizational skills and a keen eye for detail, facility with mainstream word-processing, spreadsheet, database, communications, and Internet browsing software, website design (e.g., HTML and CGI scripting) experience, desktop publishing and/or graphical design skills, and a solid sense of humor.

Benefits

In general, internships at Brandon & Associates are unpaid positions.

Contact

Robert M. Brandon & Associates
1730 Rhode Island Avenue, N.W.
Suite 712
Washington, D.C. 20036

Phone: 202-331-1550
Fax: 202-331-1663
E-mail: main@robertbrandon.com
URL: http://www.robertbrandon.com

Schwartz & Associates

General Information

A.E. Schwartz & Associates is a Boston-based training and consulting organization. Established in 1982, the company presently have eight part-time employees and several hundred external contributors. Internships focus on the development and growth of A.E. Schwartz & Associates Web site http://www.aeschwartz.com and the company's free commercial website; http://www.trainingconsortium.com. The website is dedicated to the advancement of the training, consulting and speaking industries and requires computer literate interns who can handle the demands of developing, marketing, selling and maintaining a website.

Internships Available

Internet/WWW—developing and maintaining the web sites utilizing HTML, CGI, PERL, Java Script and related programs. Corresponding with end-users to provide information, answer questions, partnerships, and solutions. Researching and installing new software/hardware products to expand current resources. Converting and constructing new databases for sales tracking. Compiling databases to coordinate with website traffic and managing on-line registration and content. Converting and utilizing word processing software packages and Internet software. Managing corporate e-mailing with auto responders.

Graphic Design—from webpages to conference slideshows to promotional flyers, image is a crucial part of the business package. Interns with an interest in design will be able to create and realize new visual concepts for the Internet sites and advertising materials. Interns are involved in the final step in the writing process, formatting workbooks or handout information for desktop publishing and adding graphics. Graphic Design Responsibilities include: creating new design concepts, overheads, manuals, articles, advertisements and newsletters. Designing flyers, book covers, sales materials, catalog and exhibit materials. Utilizing desktop publishing applications for the layout and design of training materials, presentations and publications. Designing specialty and promotional items. Providing camera-ready output, and overseeing the printing process. Animating computer-displayed slide presentations.

Benefits

Transportation stipend. Compensation contingent upon type of projects and quality of work. Potential part-time/full-time employment upon completion of internship. Students may receive academic credit.

Contact

http://www.aeschwartz.com

Sendmail, Inc.

General Information

Sendmail develops and markets commercial products and services for ISPs. Sendmail is developing a complete line of Internet mail server products based on Sendmail, one of the Internet's Mail Transfer Agents (MTA). Sendmail believes that strong marketing is key to the success of the product line and company.

Internships Available

The company has various internship opportunities to participate in several marketing communications projects during the summer. Learn about marketing in an Internet startup environment. Principal duties and responsibilities: Marketing Intranet Development—work on the marketing intranet using HTML to enhance the effectiveness of the Sendmail Sales organization. Responsible for pushing out new materials and other HTML and graphical design duties. Partner Extranet Development—responsible for defining and implementing a Partner Extranet. Work with a marketing firm to design overall look and feel. Post material targeted for this project. Web Traffic Analysis—maintain weekly logs of Sendmail's Web site traffic and advertising promotions. Conduct analyses toward identifying high traffic site segments, effectiveness of promotions, and site optimization strategies. Lead Management and Target Marketing—lead generation and tracking. Using a filemaker database the intern is responsible for recording new contacts from trade shows, the web registration form and from incoming questions from info@sendmail.com. Updating these records with contact status notes collected from the Sales organization will also be important. Be responsible for researching companies on the FTP logs and preparing summary descriptions for target marketing and sales activities. Competitive Analysis— select one key competitor and be responsible for conducting a full analysis to determine Sendmail's competitive differentiation. The resulting report should include identification of feature/functions, strengths, weaknesses, related statistics and recommendations for positioning against that competitor. Requirements: Proficient with HTML and some Graphical Design, exceptional organizational and analytical skills, experience with database administration, excellent written and verbal skills, very good interpersonal skills, with a track record of working closely with colleagues on team projects, first year MBA candidate (optional).

Benefits
Paid and unpaid internships.

Contact
Recruiting
Sendmail
6603 Shellmound St.
Emeryville, CA 94608

Phone: 510-594-5400
Fax: 510-594-5412
E-mail: jobs@sendmail.com
URL: http://www.sendmail.com

Skywalker Sound

General Information

Skywalker Sound is George Lucas' audio post production company located at Skywalker Ranch in Marin County, California. Films mixed at Skywalker Sound, and its predecessor Sprockets Systems, have won 11 Academy Awards for movie sound or sound effects editing.

Internship Available

The Lucas Digital Ltd. internship program is designed to expose students to various aspects of the entertainment industry. Skywalker Sound offers internship positions in the areas of sound. The internship application deadlines are as follows: Winter internship applications due September 13 and Summer internship applications due by March 1. Applicants who are selected for the program will be notified approximately 2 weeks before the start of the session.

Benefits

The Summer program is full-time and paid minimum wage. College credit.

Contact

Lucas Digital, Ltd. LLC
Internships
P.O. Box 2459
San Rafael, CA 94912

URL: http://www.ilm-jobs.com

Smarter Living, Inc.

General Information

Smarter Living is a free, online consumer community, publishing, and marketing company that provides members with up-to-date guides on using the Internet to save money on travel and shopping. Smarter Living membership is free and entitles Internet users to additional savings on a variety of goods, ranging from car rentals to books. The company's recognition in the media includes The New York Times, Newsweek, The Wall Street Journal, Good Morning America, US News & World Report, Money Magazine and newspapers throughout the country.

Internship Available

Web Design Intern—the primary responsibility of the web design intern is thinking through how Smarter Living can best serve its membership and advertisers through the design of its web pages and e-mails. This includes designing the overall architecture of the web site and the actual creation of web pages. The intern will be expected to be a critical member of the project team, providing insights into all aspects of the business. Job Requirements: Smart, creative, and motivated self-starter who wants to play a leading role in charting the future of a growing company. Experience with HTML, graphic design and layout, and the development of images in electronic formats is essential. Familiarity with a UNIX environment and understanding of perl and cgi scripting, HTML 4.0, Javascript, and CSS are pluses. Full- or part-time, competitive salary or college credit.

Benefits

Possibly paid internship.

Contact:

Smarter Living, Inc.
432 Columbia St.
Cambridge, MA 02141.

Fax: 617-374-8880
E-mail: Careers@SmarterLiving.com
URL: http://www.smarterliving.com

Soap Opera Digest

General Information

Soap Opera Digest is a source of soap opera news and information, with all the latest news about daytime dramas updated daily. SOD Online offers news, stories and interviews that differ from its print sister.

Internships Available

Chat and Message Boards Monitor for SoapOperaDigest.com. Responsibilities would include engendering a community, setting the verbal tone, and cleaning out the message boards. College credit compensation. Likely monitor candidates must have prior experience using web message boards and chatting on the web.

Benefits

Time commitment is approximately 5 hours a week. This is an unpaid internship, and there are no stipends. Interested candidates should send résumé and cover letter by e-mail

Contact

Jessica Heitman
New Media Assistant.
SoapOperaDigest.com
200 Madison Avenue
8th Floor NY, NY 10016

Phone: 212-448-4728
Fax: 212-252-7725
E-mail: Jessica_Heitman@PrimediaMags.com
URL: http://www.SoapOperaDigest.com

SOL Design FX

General Information

Currently employees, SOL Design is a small boutique company using a combinations of high-tech and traditional methods to create designs and effects works for advertising companies. The company's clients include Janet Jackson, Puff Daddy, and Smashing Pumpkins.

Internships Available

Positions including internships and volunteer training programs.

Benefits

Unpaid internships.

Contact

Michele Hubbs
SOL Design FX
120 Broadway, Ste. 260
Santa Monica, CA 90401

Phone: 310-453-6311
Fax: 310-453-6431

E-mail: michele@soldesignfx.com
URL: http://www.soldesignfx.com

Southern Exposure

General Information

An artist-run organization, Southern Exposure reaches out to diverse audiences, and serves as a forum and resource center that provides support to the Bay Area's arts and educational communities.

Internship Available

Southern Exposure staff members provide thorough orientation, training, evaluation and recognition for interns. Internships are offered in the following areas: arts administration, AIE, live events, exhibition coordination, curatorial, membership, and fund-raising.

Benefits
All internships are unpaid and require a minimum of six hours per week and a six month commitment. Shorter summer internships are also available.

Contact
Southern Exposure
401 Alabama Street
San Francisco, CA 94110

Phone: 415-863-2141
Fax: 415-863-1841
E-mail: soex@soex.org
URL: http://www.soex.org

StandUp For Kids

General Information
Empower homeless and street kids toward lifelong personal growth through a national on-the-streets program. Create in these youth a caring and belief in themselves through open straightforward counseling and educational programs, thereby, attaining the life skills necessary to become effective members of the community.

Internships Available
WWW Assistant—this internship is for a web site designer to assist in building an informative and educational site. The organization needs several designers, Web builders, and HTML writers to keep the site current. Skills: Web page design, computer training, graphic design.

Benefits
Unpaid internship. College credits.

Contact
Linda J. Ada
StandUp For Kids
Post Office Box 121
Chula Vista, California, 80204

Phone: 619-585-0063
Fax: 888-453-1647
E-mail: LindaA@standupforkids.org
URL: http://www.standupforkids.org

Sunbow Entertainment

General Information

They are a production company that makes animated children's television. The New York office consists of the management team and Los Angeles office is where actual animation production is done. Sunbow Entertainment develops an idea, produces it to sell, and distributes it all over the world, then markets it and merchandises it.

Internships Available

Sunbow Entertainment hires from within the organization. Three of the current full time employees began as interns. Duties includes faxing, copying, filing, and also an opportunity to be involved in each department's projects. Interns are department specific or "float" between departments as needed and get experience in everything the departments do. Send (fax or mail) a cover letter and résumé detailing interest in Sunbow and list background and prior experience.

Benefits

This is a non-paid internship. The internship at Sunbow assistance is housing or job placement. College credits only.

Contact
Nicole Frydman
Internship Coordinator
Sunbow Entertainment
100 Fifth Avenue, 3rd Floor
New York, NY 10011

Phone: 212-886-4900
Fax: 212-366-4242

SWIFTT, Inc.

General Information

SWIFTT began in 1988 by Mayor John MacNamara to improve the community and business climate in southwest Rockford. The goals are to promote economic and neighborhood development in order to benefit area residents and businesses and the community-at-large, and to provide and develop a leadership base.

Internships Available

Advertising Manager—skills in graphic design, web page maintenance, typing. Report to the Marketing Director on a daily or weekly basis for the report of ideas, projects, future ambitions. The qualified candidate must be a team player, professional presence, and detail oriented and organized. This position is unpaid, but is available for college credit through an accredited school within this major or related field. Hours worked will be 20 - 40 hours per week depending on financial criteria. Will receive assistance for paid employment in the area. Maintain office environment attitude and work with Marketing Director on advertising projects. Obtain references for subsequent job hunts.

Benefits

Unpaid internship.

Contact
Maine Prince
St. Elizabeth's Community Center
1536 South Main Street
Rockford, Illinois, 61102

Fax: 815-965-9836
E-mail: proplaya@earthlink.net

Tribune Broadcasting

General Information

A division of Tribune Media Services, providing information and entertainment products to newspapers and electronic media. TMS syndicate and license comics, features and opinion columns, television listings, Internet, online and wire services, and advertising networks.

Internships Available

The Tribune Broadcasting Creative Services Group offers internship opportunities in the Creative Services area.

Benefits

Internships are non-paid and for college credit only.

Contact

Jackie Dickson
Tribune Creative Services Group
524 Armour Circle, NE
Atlanta, Georgia 30324

Fax: 404-874-8603
URL: http://www.tribune.com

Tribune Media Services

General Information

TMS is a provider of information and entertainment products to newspapers and electronic media. TMS syndicates and licenses comics, features and opinion columns, television listings, Internet, online and wire services, and advertising networks.

Internship Available

Tribune Media Services will be offering a variety of internship opportunities every summer. Internships are available in the technical, editorial, marketing, database and finance groups.

Benefits

Unpaid internships.

Contact

Colleen Los
Tribune Media Services
435 N. Michigan Ave.
Suite 510
Chicago, IL 60611

Phone: 312-222-9100
E-mail: clos@tribune.com
URL: http://www.tribune.com

TUV Productions rrr by ABC of Film

General Information

A motion-picture-making-company working in the world of cinematography, animation and movie-making, computer-graphics web design and media.

Internships Available

Internship positions are available at the TUV Productions rrr by ABC of FILM. Need strong background in graphic design, Flash applications, and art. This position requires 4 or more years of college education, working knowledge of the web and graphic design is a must.

Benefits
Unpaid internship. Opportunity for college credits.

Contact
TUV Productions rrr by ABC of Film
4410 Clayburn Dr.
Indianapolis, IN 46268

Phone: 317-872-FILM
Fax: 317-872 -3456
E-mail: cinemaparadiso@netzero.net

Universal Studios

General Information
Universal Studios is a diversified entertainment company in motion pictures, recreation, television and home-based entertainment. Universal Studios owns Universal Music Group. Core businesses are Universal Pictures, Universal Studios Recreation Group, Universal Television and Networks Group, Universal Studios Consumer Products Group and Spencer Gifts, DAPY, GLOW!. In addition, the Corporate division has a number of other opportunities including: Universal Studios Online, Universal Studios Information Technology (IT) and Universal Studios Operations Group.

Internships Available
Interns gain real world experience while learning what a career at Universal Studios might hold in store. Internships at Universal vary. Music Group— music interns can choose from any of the companies many labels to live music on stage. Universal Family and Home Entertainment, Universal Cartoon Studios, Online Service group and the New Media Division offers internship opportunities.

Benefits

Paid and unpaid internships. Possible college credits. Free CDs, videos, T-shirts depending on the division and location of the internship.

Contact

For opportunities with Universal Pictures, Universal Studios Recreational Group, Universal City Hollywood, Universal Creative, Universal Studios Japan, Universal Music Group, Universal Television and Networks Group, Universal Studios Consumer Products, Universal Studios Online, Universal Studios Operations Group, and Universal Studios, either e-mail jobs@unistudios.com or mail a résumé to:

Universal Studios
National Résumé Processing Center
Internet
P.O. Box 385
Burlington, MA 01803

For opportunities with Universal Studios Escape (which includes Universal Studios Florida and Universal Studios Islands of Adventure theme parks, Universal Studios City Walk, and resort hotels), send résumé to:

Universal City Florida
Human Resources Department
1000 Universal Studios Plaza
Orlando, Florida 32819-7610

Fax: 407-224-7987
URL: http://www.universalstudios.com

Universal Systems Inc. [USI]

General Information

Established in early 1990, USI has twelve offices throughout the United States and Europe that are involved in work management, e-business solutions, and developing complex systems integration. The company's e.POWER product architecture is involved with imaging, document management, records management, workflow and the Internet.

Internship Available

USI is creating the software, integrating the systems and building the applications for vertical industries, Intern/Research Assistant—research 3rd party software products to support USI's e.Power product line. Research competitive products in the document management and workflow industry and assist in managing the Product Organization's intranet site. Responsibilities also include the installation of software packages, set up of the infrastructure, building working demos/prototypes and product write-ups. The ideal candidate will be taking college classes toward BSCS degree and have experience with development in MS Windows (i.e., VB, Delphi); familiarity with SQL, 3rd Party Toolkits (i.e., VBX, OCX) and Windows SDK; HTML knowledge; Microsoft FrontPage and Microsoft IIS web server experience. Experience with Visual Basic, Delphi, Oracle, SQL Server, Messaging (MS Exchange, Lotus Notes), Internet/Intranet/Web Development is desired. Graphics Artist skills are also desired.

Benefits

Paid internship.

Contact

USI
14585 Avion Parkway
99PSD-Intern
Chantilly, VA 20151

Fax: 703-222-7222
E-mail: hr_employment@usiva.com.
URL: http://www.usiva.com

Virginia Museum of Fine Arts

General Information

Established in 1936. Virginia Museum of Fine Arts is a state supported museum collecting original works of fine art.

Internship Available

Photography intern—responsibilities include assisting staff of the museum with documenting the art works.

Benefits

Unpaid internship. Possible college credit exchange.

Contact

Virginia Museum of Fine Arts
2800 Grove Avenue
Richmond, VA 23221-2466

Phone 804-367-0844
Fax: 804-367-9393
E-mail: webmaster@vmfa.state.va.us

Wadsworth Atheneum

General Information

Founded in 1842 by Daniel Wadsworth, the museum contains portraits and sculpture, American landscape and history paintings by prominent artists such as Thomas Cole, Frederic Church and John Trumbull, who were friends of Daniel Wadsworth.

Internship Available

The Internship program is designed for undergraduates and graduate students and is tailored to meet individual needs. In addition to major projects in one of the museum's departments, interns participate in weekly museum studies seminars. These seminars provide an overview of the Wadsworth's departments and of the ways in which these departments interact within the museum. Spring and Fall interns work for 12 hours each week (120 hours per semester). Summer interns work 20 hours each week for 8 to 10 weeks. Each intern determines with his/her advisor what requirements must be met for academic credit. Internships are available in the following areas: Curatorial, Development, Design and Installation, Photographic Services, Business Office, The Museum Shop, Education, Library, Registrar, Membership, and Marketing.

Benefits

Internships do not carry a stipend, and living arrangements are the responsibility of the intern. The museum offers advice about lodging and transportation. Students are assigned to work in specific departments according to their interests and skills.

Contact
Internship Program
Wadsworth Atheneum
600 Main Street
Hartford, CT 06103

Phone: 860-278-2670
Fax: 860-527-0803
E-mail: info@wadsworthatheneum.org
URL: http://www.wadsworthatheneum.org

Walt Disney Feature Animation

General Information
The Walt Disney Animation Florida Internship Program is an in-depth work experience in animation, including instructional activities, tutorials, practical workshops, studio assignments and production experience. Tutorial within the Animation Studio, located in the Disney-MGM Studios Theme Park, traditional animation techniques and skills is presented by experienced professionals.

Internships Available

This concentrated program is designed to give interns insight into the animation process. Classes - Interns will attend scheduled discussions on topics pertaining to the basic principles of animation, production techniques and studio processes. Lectures - Interns attend scheduled presentations relating to specific animation procedures, history of animation and contemporary motion picture advances. Screenings - Interns attend weekly screenings of animation and live action classics, structured for awareness of the problem solving necessary to achieve successful results in narrative and cinematic style, continuity and performance. Studio Assignments - In the Animation Studio, the artist's greatest tool is the ability to draw well. Drawing Skills -Emphasis is given to developing the interns' fundamental ability to draw for animated film through observational studies, action analysis, and traditional figure drawing sessions. Drawing Techniques for Animation Production - Assignments to develop the artist's skills in order to draw characters consistent with model sheets, developing line quality and shape/ movement continuity. Production In-between - Assignments in working with a production group on actual animation sequences. The artist will in-between and clean up drawings based on timing notes and animation keys. Individual Animation Assignments - Basic principles of animation, using studio facilities, are developed in a project format in order to see how interns can creatively produce a small piece of animation. Assignments will be based on the following progressive steps, each of which must be approved by supervising production personnel before going onto the next: proposal, thumbnail, storyboard, key pose and rough in-between, key clean-up. Background/layout assignments vary but also develop in similarly progressive phases. Requirements: a résumé is absolutely essential. Portfolios are returned if a résumé is not submitted at the same time. A brief letter outlining area of interest (character animation, background, layout, etc.) is also important.

Benefits

Relocation Assistance: Walt Disney World Co. provides a travel allowance check to students who drive to Orlando for the Internship. This allowance is intended to offset the transportation costs from the city of origin to Walt Disney World. The student receives this check during the first week of work. In lieu of driving, a one-way coach flight to Orlando can be arranged by the Walt Disney Travel Company. Upon successful completion of the program, the Company will, once again, provide benefits to assist with returning. Housing: Vista Way is an apartment complex located near the Walt Disney World Vacation Kingdom. Students share fully furnished, two and three bedroom apartments which include linens, housewares and telephone service. A mail pick-up center is located at the complex office. Rent payments, which include utilities and transportation to and from work, will be paid in the form of a weekly payroll deduction. There is an option of arranging other housing. These details must be completed prior to the beginning of the semester. Walt Disney World and Disney Feature Animation cannot make private arrangements on behalf of individuals.

Contact

Walt Disney World Professional Staffing
P.O. Box 10,090
Lake Buena Vista, FL 32820

Phone: 407-828-3110
URL: http://www.disney.com

Walt Disney Feature Animation
Training Department
960 North Cypress Drive
Bay Lake, FL 32830

Walt Disney Feature Animation
CGI Training Program
Artist Recruitment
500 South Buena Vista Street
Burbank, CA 91521-4866.

Additional Information on Portfolio

All work must be submitted in a traditional portfolio. No rolled samples. No more than 24 X 30 inches. All work should be mounted on heavy paper or behind plastic on standard portfolio pages. Mounting on illustration board and matting is not necessary or recommended. If pastel, chalk or charcoal works are presented, they must be fixed and/or mounted behind plastic. The artist's name or initials must be on each page or sample. Portfolios should not exceed 25 pages of work. A sketch book, short video tape or portfolio page with several drawings are considered one page. Please do not send stretched and/or framed work. Slides and/or photocopies are acceptable, especially for color work. Whenever possible, life drawing should be presented in original medium. Video tapes should be clear and no longer than four minutes. A table of contents identifying each sequence and the artist's responsibility on that sequence must be included. (NTSC format please. VHS or 3/4 inch tapes are fine.) Portfolios not meeting these requirements may not be evaluated.

Guidelines: Traditional Portfolio

A good selection of carefully rendered figure drawings using line to emphasize volume and structure. Also include sketch books or loose sketches (mounted) of animals and humans in motion done in quick gesture style. Generally, drawings should be from live subjects. Do not copy photographs. Samples of cartooning skills and drawings from imagination are appropriate but should not comprise a major part of portfolio work. If interested in story sketch, layout, background or effects, approximately half of the portfolio should reflect appropriate art. Animation Services Portfolio: An Animation Services portfolio is much the same as the traditional portfolio except that there would be additional examples of cartooning, and finished illustration, especially involving examples related to video games, CD ROM graphics, etc. In this case, life drawing should only take up about one-half the portfolio with the rest being more specific work. It is important to note on the portfolio it is for Animation Services. Things NOT to send: Copies of Disney (or other studio's) characters. Comic strip or comic book work. (A small sampling can be included if applicant is interested in layout.) Super hero, and science/fantasy illustrations. Graphic, poster, industrial and advertising design. Clay animation models or sculpture. Textile, jewelry, or three-dimensional design work. When to Submit: Walt Disney Feature Animation Florida reviews portfolios on a monthly basis, though the main portfolio reviews for the Intern Program are generally scheduled for late March or early April. It is from this evaluation that final candidates are chosen for the intern semester. Those interested in the Summer Intern Program make sure portfolios are in prior to the April 1st target deadline. Additionally, if submitting during the year, do it well in advance of the major review so that feedback can be received in order to better prepare the portfolio for re-submission.

Wave Works Digital Media

General Information
A new media company with a primary focus in creating sound tracks for television and radio commercial spots. The company is also equipped to do post production video effects and 3D computer animation.

Internship Available
Wave Works offers internships in sound, new media graphics and post production.

Benefits
Unpaid internships. College credits. Successful interns are considered for employment within the company

Contact
Wave Works
1100 N. Glebe Rd. 100
Arlington, VA 22201
Phone: 703-527-1100
Fax: 703-527-1308

900 Second St. NE Suite 309
Washington, DC 20002
Phone: 202-842-7678
Fax: 202-842-0019

E-mail: psmith@waveworks.net
URL: http://www.waveworks.net

WB56

General Information

All internships at WB56 are hands-on, and are for students who are serious and dedicated to the field of journalism and communications. Students are required to make a commitment of at least 16 hours per week or more. This may include some nights and weekends for news or sports.

Internships Available

Internships are available in: Programming, Promotion, Finance, Graphics, Public Relations, Community Affairs and Online Development, News, Sports, Health, Political or Weather. WB56 Internship Areas:

Community Affairs—research program topics; assist production staff with all aspects of production; write copy/produce community calendars or other short forms; assist in pre-screening and scheduling program guests, creative input required, including story ideas; assist with coordination of music; assist executive producer with daily tasks; answer phones, viewer mail, etc.; coordinate program materials for show's director.

Graphics / Art Department—desktop publishing experience is helpful; assist in preparation of mechanicals for print promotion; compile data for filing; assist art director in all aspects of set/graphics design by assuming projects; learn Art Directors' and Graphic Artists' approach to daily problems and deadlines; observe creative process for on-air promotion and be able to work independently; hands on involvement and exposure to graphics for

News Department, promotional materials, one sheets for the Sales Department, etc.

The Ten O'clock News—telephone interviewing, coverage and screening; information gathering, research and logging; in-the-field interviews and assistance; occasional courier duties (minimal); general newsroom assistance and Assignment desk coverage; limited production assistance; general office assistance: telephones, filing, sorting mail.

Online Development—this is an editorial writing position, not a technical coding or graphic design position. Requires good writing skills and knowledge of how to surf the web, not necessary to know HTML. Take part in daily content-development for the station's sites on the Web (wb56.com); help evaluate which news stories to put online; produce at least one story or TV show update each day; learn to capture video from news tapes; assist in responding to viewer mail.

Political—general office support (i.e. phones, filing, sorting mail); greet and escort guests to studio/set; possible library research on show topics; possible location shooting with photographer; possible assistance for man-in-the-street interviews; assist talent in news gathering for nightly news; generation of letters and press releases; receive weekly assignments from talent via telephone.

Programming—answer viewer phone calls and correspondence; learn computer applications for programming; learn who and what syndicators are; learn how programs are selected and scheduled; learn market demographics and ratings periods; possibility of sitting in on programming meetings; learn what various station/departmental reports mean.

Promotions—write voice-overs, movie opens, closes, etc.; observe on-air promotion production; observe edit sessions; write and produce at least one 30 seconds and one 10 seconds movie promo; participate in at least one outside promotion event; earn how to prepare spot order logs; assist with special mailings ; assist in updating and compiling media lists.

Public Relations / Marketing—assist with research, typing and distribution of press releases; develop and maintain key press contacts; ensure programming is publicized; assist with coordination of special events and trade shows; maintain press clip file; maintain press kits, making sure information is current; assist with designing sponsorship opportunities; assist with drafting sales one-sheets.

Weather—information gathering, and research; forecasting techniques ; forecast events; infield, on location, observations of major storms (if applicable); assist in preparation of nightly weathercast for on-air meteorologist; provide general office assistance; learn graphic and meteorological systems, including Kavouras, SGI, Doppler, Difax and remote sensing equipment.

Sports—logging of nightly games; in-the-field assistance with various sports assignments and Live-shots (attend some sporting events); assistance with interviews and preparation of stories for broadcast; editing and writing of game highlights (with assistance); general assistance with nightly sportscasts.

Benefits
Non-paid internship students must receive college credits, or do the internship as a special for-credit project with a class.

Contact
Ms. Sandy Averill
Internship Coordinator
WB56
75 Morrissey Blvd.
Boston, MA 02125

Fax: 617-265-2538

WBBM TV (CBS)

General Information

A CBS affiliate serving the Chicago area.

Internships Available

CBS 2 Chicago (CBS Owned and Operated) News Department has internships in the following areas: Assignment Desk, Investigative Unit, Sports and Weather. First-hand experience working in all areas of the newsroom.

Benefits

College credit for the internship. This is an unpaid internship.

Contact

Lissa Druss
Assignment Editor
WBBM-TV/CBS
630 N. McClurg Ct.
Chicago, IL 60611

Phone: 312-944-6000
URL: http://www.cbs2chicago.com

WDBJ 7

General Information

WDBJ-TV's studio first signed on the air in 1955 in Roanoke, Virginia. In 1969 Schurz Communications of South Bend, Indiana purchased WDBJ 7 from the Times-World Corporation. WDBJ 7 operates local newsrooms in Lynchburg, Blacksburg, Danville and Richmond.

Internships Available

Internships are available in News Reporting, News Photography, Sports, Production, Sales, Promotion, Graphics and Engineering. News Photojournalist—entry level position for News Photographer to shoot and edit videotape news stories. Experience with broadcast video cameras and editors desired.

Benefits

WDBJ Television offers unpaid internships to college-level students majoring in broadcasting, communications or a related field. Gain practical experience in areas of interest, as well as an overview of the station in general.

Contact

Personnel Manager
WDBJ Television, Inc.
P. O. Box 7
Roanoke, VA 24022-0007

The Weber Group

General Information

A public relations firm specializing in immediate, interactive and information-driven new media. The Weber Group works in Marketing PR, Brand and Reputation Management, Global Public Relations Management, Public Affairs, Investor Relations, and Media and Presentation Training. The Weber Group's Emerging Business Practice offers an opportunity to work with some of the high-growth technology companies, learning how to get a new company off the ground and into the big leagues. The Enterprise Practice provides direct experience in running strategic-level communications programs for technology and consumer technology brands.

Internships Available

An entree into the business world. Offers the experience to develop and qualify media lists, research media opportunities via the Internet, track client and industry coverage, and work as an integral part of the accounting teams.

Benefits

This is a paid position, available for full-time college students (minimum of 15 hours per week) as well as recent college graduates.

Contact
The Weber Group
P.O. Box 439
Burlington, MA 01803

Fax: 800-657-4126
E-mail: webergroup@webhire.com
URL: http://www.webhire.com

WFAA TV (ABC)

General Information
ABC affiliate in Dallas and producers of the "Good Morning Texas" show.

Internships Available
Various production internships.

Benefits
Non-paid internships are available. Students must be getting college credit for the internship.

Contact
Good Morning Texas
Blanca Salazar
606 Young Street
Dallas, Texas 75202

Phone: 214-977-6493
Fax: 214-977-6550
E mail: gmt@wfaa.com

WFOR-TV CBS 4 News

General Information
WFOR-TV has served South Florida in many ways since first signing on the air in 1967, as WCIX-TV, owned by Coral Television.

The local owners moved the license from Islamorada, in the Florida Keys, to the mainland, to serve more people. Now, WFOR is preparing to transmit a digital, High-Definition TV signal. They are currently building a new transmission facility to transmit digital pictures and CD quality sound to South Florida.

Internships Available

Internships are available in television news. This is an opportunity to: work at the CBS4 News assignment desk; learn the internal workings of the newsroom; participate in the preparation of CBS4 News broadcasts; work with reporters and producers; go with reporters on assignment; have access to tools needed for eventual job hunting.

Benefits

Unpaid internship. Opportunity for college credits.

Contact

Manager, Assignments
WFOR-TV
8900 NW 18th Terrace
Miami, FL 33172

URL: http://www.wfor.cbsnow.com

WHP-TV/UPN 15 WLYH

General Information

Established in 1953 WHP-TV is an affiliate of CBS in Central Pennsylvania.

Internships Available

WHP-TV/UPN 15 WLYH Production Intern—must be able to lift 50 lbs., and available to work at least 15 hours per week on a flexible schedule; have course work in broadcast or related field.

Benefits

Non-paid internship.

Contact
John Wertz
WHP-TV/UPN 15 WLYH
3300 N. Sixth St.
Harrisburg, PA 17110

URL: http://www.whptv.com/

WMAR TV (ABC)

General Information
WMAR-TV, the ABC affiliate in Baltimore.

Internships Available
Areas include, News, Sales, Promotion, Production, Graphics, and Public
Service/Relations.

Benefits
Unpaid internship for college credits only.

Contact
Brenda Mustian
Internship Coordinator
WMAR-TV
6400 York Road
Baltimore, MD 21212

WNBC

General Information
WNBC offers internship positions for applicants interested in all departments
of the broadcasting television business.

Internships Available
Students have the opportunity to work in sports, weather, news, promotion,
public relations, community relations, sales, research and marketing, and

engineering. Internships are also available at "News 4's" Long Island and New Jersey bureaus.

Benefits
The experiences are varied and offer the student who is academically prepared an opportunity to learn the television market. Offered each semester. This is an non-paid internship; students must receive college credit for the experience.

Contact
Internship Coordinator
WNBC Employee Relations
Room 602
30 Rockefeller Plaza
New York, NY 10112

E-mail: wnbc@nbc.com

WNDU-TV

General Information
WNDU-TV is owned by the University of Notre Dame, but it is not a student-operated educational station. WNDU is the professionally staffed NBC affiliate in the South Bend/Elkhart DMA. Golden Dome Productions (a division of the company) is a full service production house offering services ranging from web pages and interactive CD-ROM programs to surgical instruction videos to satellite teleconferencing and documentary productions.

Internships Available
Because of its relationship with Notre Dame, WNDU offers a variety of student internships in all phases of broadcast television and video production. During the academic year (August-May), most of the internships are reserved for students at the University of Notre Dame. Most positions are open to qualified applicants from other schools—especially during the summer (May-August).

Benefits

Unpaid internship, students must receive college credits.

Contact

Karen Heisler
Coordinator, Internship Program
P.O. Box 1616
South Bend, IN 46634

E-mail: Gary.J.Sieber.1@nd.edu

WNEP-TV 16

General Information

WNEP's news operation is fully computerized, with a Dynatech NewStar system. All news interns receive computer instruction and are expected to become adept at using the computer system. WNEP-TV also produces a weekly program titled "Pennsylvania Outdoor Life", which is aimed at individuals who hunt, fish, camp, and do other outdoor activities. Interns with Pennsylvania Outdoor Life try various specialties: filming, writing, post-production, etc. The News Department requires interns to be either seniors or entering their senior year. WNEP-TV News is a 24 hour-a-day operation, so an individual's schedules may rotate among day, night, and overnight shifts. News interns may not have any other scheduled classes or outside employment.

Internships Available

WNEP-TV accepts interns in general categories of news, production, and engineering. News internships may be in meteorology, sports reporting, sports videography, news videography/editing, newscast producing, consumer reporting, and general assignment reporting. Production interns work under the supervision of producers and directors in preparing local programs, promotions, and commercials. Opportunities include technical directing, audio, Chyron Scribe, CMX editing, and field production. An internship is also available in Electronic Graphics. Graphics interns assist staff artists in preparing news graphics, commercial artwork, and 3-D rendering. Engineering students have the opportunity to learn Master Control operation, satellite news gathering techniques, troubleshooting of E.N.G. equipment and systems.

Benefits

All internships must be taken for credit; three credits minimum. Interns receive no pay. The student must arrange housing. The student must possess a valid driver's license. Internships are scheduled concurrently with the student's school calendar. Scheduling in non-News departments is worked out to the mutual satisfaction of the student and the WNEP-TV department head. However, internships that might conflict with scheduled classes are not encouraged. WNEP-TV does not accept "part-time" internships; all interns are expected to work 40 hours a week for no less than 12 weeks.

Contact

Len Modzelesky
Internship Coordinator
c/o WNEP-TV 16
16 Montage Mountain Road
Moosic, PA 18507

Women Make Movies, Inc.

General Information

Women Make Movies is a multicultural, multiracial, non-profit media arts organization which facilitates the production, promotion, distribution and exhibition of independent films and videotapes by and about women. Women Make Movies was established in 1972 to address the under representation and misrepresentation of women in the media industry. The organization provides services to both users and makers of film and video programs, with a special emphasis on supporting work by women of color. Women Make Movies facilitates the development of feminist media through Distribution Services and a Production Assistance Program.

Internship Available

Distribution Assistant—duties include updating databases and mailing lists, maintaining distribution files, upkeep of in-house video library, mailing promotional materials, and maintaining promotional files. Desire individuals with an interest in independent media, excellent communication and organizational skills and computer literacy in IBM and/or Macintosh systems.

Promotions Assistant—duties include assisting sales and marketing staff with outreach to community based and academic organizations, assisting with production and mailing of promotional materials, and doing on-line research. Desire individual with excellent communication skills, knowledge of the Internet and/or desktop publishing and computer literacy in IBM and/or Macintosh systems.

General Office Intern—duties include updating and maintaining lists on computer database, general office duties, and responding to general information requests. Desire individuals with computer literacy on IBM and Macintosh systems, and excellent writing, interpersonal and communication skills.

Artist's Services Assistant—work with the Production Assistance Program researching and updating grant files and other filmmaker resources. Assist with management of project files and program databases. Assist Media Workshops. Desire individuals with excellent organizational and communication skills, knowledge of IBM computer systems and knowledge of production.

Graphic Production/Website Maintenance Assistant—duties include producing one-sheets and other promotional pieces from templates. Desire individuals with an interest in independent media, excellent communication and organizational skills, and knowledge of Macintosh based Quark Express and PC-based Front Page. Interns are asked to work a minimum 15 hours per week. Duration is flexible to meet university requirements, but a minimum commitment of three months is optimal. Interns are required to sign an agreement outlining the duration and schedule of their internship.

Benefits
Local travel reimbursement (up to $9 weekly), free workshop attendance (spring and fall), access to screen films/tapes in their collection, and invitations to screenings and receptions. An internship stipend of $150 per month is available for Website Maintenance Assistant with skills in Front Page.

Contact
Women Make Movies, Inc.
462 Broadway, 5th Floor
New York, NY 10013

Phone: 212-925-0606
Fax: 212-925-2052
URL: http://www.wmm.com

World Children's Transplant Fund

General Information
The company's mission is to provide for life-saving organ transplantation to children of the world. WCTF helps supply the technology, the training and the teaching needed to establish pediatric organ transplantation capabilities in foreign and domestic areas that lack these services. In time, this will enable children of foreign lands to remain in their native environment with family and friends while awaiting the transplant process. The demand for transplantable organs exceeds availability. By introducing transplant technology and training to the countries that lack such services, WCTF helps establish self-sufficient pediatric transplant services in countries where the need is the greatest, while alleviating the additional burden foreign transplant recipients place on already overextended organ procurement lists in the United States.

Internships Available

Web master—to upgrade and maintain organization's web site.

Benefits

Unpaid internship

Contact

Michael Reid, Ed.D., Executive Director
World Children's Transplant Fund
6000 Ventura Blvd., Suite 103
Encino, CA 91436

Phone: 818-905-9283
Fax: 818-905-9315

E-mail: mreid@wctf.org
URL: http://www.wctf.org

WPMT-TV Fox 43

General Information

Partners of Tribune, a media company in television and radio broadcasting, publishing, education and interactive ventures.

Internship Available

WPMT has internship opportunities in the following departments: Art, Promotion, Public Affairs, Sales, Programming and News.

Benefits

WPMT can provide a meaningful look at the real world of broadcasting. A FOX43 internship is an opportunity to do hands-on promotion, art and graphics, video, station events and complement academic tenure with practical day-to-day experience. Internships at FOX43 are unpaid, however the station considers mileage reimbursement at a fixed rate for certain students whose travel is excessive.

Contact
WPMT FOX43
Internship Opportunities
2005 S. Queen St.
York, PA 17403

Phone: 717-843-0043
Fax: 717-843-9741
URL: http://www.fox43.com

WTOV-TV9

General Information: WTOV-TV9 is an NBC affiliate that serves the Steubenville, Ohio and Wheeling, West Virginia television market. WTOV-TV is owned and operated by STC Broadcasting, Inc. Channel 9 began it's operation on December 24, 1953 as WSTV-TV, a CBS affiliate, owned and operated by the Russ Craft/Friendly Group. In 1978, the station was sold to Ziff-Davis Broadcasting. Along with a call letter change came a change in network affiliation to NBC. In 1983, WTOV-TV was purchased by Television Station Partners L.P. and in 1996 WTOV-TV was acquired by it's present owner which also owns and operates seven other television stations. Currently employs 79 employees.

Internships Available
Various production internships are available to students pursuing a career in communications. WTOV9 internships are offered year round.

Benefits
Internships for college credits only; must be a college student and have college permission.

Contact
Sondra Nestor, Human Resources Administrator
WTOV-TV, Box 9999
Steubenville, OH 43952

URL: http://www.wtov.com/jobs.htm

WTVH-5

General Information

WTVH-5 went on the air on December 1, 1948 as WHEN-TV Channel 8. WTVH-5 is the CBS Affiliate in Syracuse, New York and is owned by Granite Broadcasting Corporation.

Internships Available

Internships are available in News, Sports, Sales and Promotion.

News—the station produces five daily newscasts Monday through Friday and two on each weekend day. The goal of the WTVH-5 News Internship program is to observe all aspects of what it takes to get news covered... to get those newscasts on the air...and to work under deadline pressure. Some of the intern responsibilities include answering phones, doing research, logging feeds, accompanying crews out in the field and helping develop story ideas. Students will work closely with all news staff, including producers, reporters and photojournalists. College students' curriculum must include one or more of the following: broadcasting, communications, journalism, or meteorology.

Sports—sports interns at WTVH-5 get practical experience in broadcast journalism. Responsibilities are important in putting a good product on the air. Duties typically include logging sporting events in the field or off television, finding footage or sound cuts off feed tapes or file tapes, assisting sports reporters in interviewing newsmakers, and editing videotape for sports files (not for broadcast). Additionally, interns participate in reviewing nightly sportscasts on WTVH-5 and its competitors. Interns gain knowledge of what is required on a daily basis to put a quality sportscast on the air.

Sales—learn the sales process and work with the Local Sales Team. Meet with clients, and learn how to put proposals together. Participate in the production of a commercial, and then see the end result on WTVH-5.

Sales Special Events and Promotion—WTVH-5 creates targeted events and other special opportunities each year for the advertising clients. Work hands-on as to plan and execute the Women's Lifestyle Expo, Kids Fest, and more. The intern also works closely with I-5, the World Wide Web site. Some Internet experience helpful.

Promotion—WTVH-5 airs dozens of commercials or "promotions", each day about their own programs. This internship includes brainstorming, writing, location scouting, and assisting in the overall production of promotional announcements for the station. Also participate in WTVH-5 events, from start to finish. The interns curriculum must include one or more of the following: Television Production, Public Relations, and Marketing or Advertising.

Benefits

WTVH-5 offers an internship program for college credit to junior, senior or graduate students in the Communications field.

Contact
Human Resources Department
WTVH-5
980 James Street
Syracuse, NY 13203

URL: http://www.wtvh.com

WTXF-FOX Philadelphia

General Information

WTXF-FOX Philadelphia's internship program provides students with the opportunity to gain practical experience in all aspects of television production.

Internships Available

WTXF-FOX Philadelphia has intern opportunities in: Public Affairs, Fox Focus, New Jersey Journal, Human Resources, Sales, Traffic, Promotion,

Investigative Team, News, Sports, Operations/Production, Planning Editor, Director Projects, Anchor/Talent Projects, Producer Projects.

Public Affairs—preparation, including copywriting of Community Update, maintenance of community leader files; topic research for special projects; Assist in community leader/group contact; assist in public service production sessions; general administrative duties.

Fox Focus—topic research; guest bookings; pre-show interviewing; assist in preparation of quarterly reports; general administrative duties.

New Jersey Journal—topic research; guest bookings; pre-show interviewing; Assist in preparation of quarterly reports; general administration.

Human Resources—learn and assist in the handling of résumés; learn and assist in the screening of job applicants and interns; assist in preparation of EEO, monthly, and various other reports; Assist with administration of employee benefits.

Sales—ratings and demographic research; Assist with sales promotion activities; assist salespersons in various aspects of account activity.

Traffic—inventory control; format programs; preparation of daily log.

Promotion—observation/orientation to promotion production; Copywriting for press releases, over credits and movie copy (dependent on skill and ability); non-linear and regular video editing of the promotions; general administrative.

Investigative Unit—undercover research and field production - overt and covert; story research; assist producers and reporter in all aspects of production and research. *News:* Story research; pre-show interviewing; maintenance of video tape library; assist producer, director and anchors in telecast; general administrative.

Sports—logging sporting events for highlight selection for air; coordinating scripts with producers and talent; updating file system of professional, college, and high school sporting events; assist photographers on remote assignments.

Operations/Production—assist staff directors in all assigned production sessions and programs, including weekend newscast; Chyron observation and training; editing observation and training; simple machine to machine cuts video editing of "Your World" segments; general administrative (program screening, format computation).

Planning Editor—assist in research and set up stories for reporters; Internet research.

Director Projects—assist in pre-production; observe directing of Ten O'clock news and FOX News on the hour cut-ins.

Anchor/Talent Projects—setting up stories; help with interviews and gathering sound; looking up file tape and researching video and script archives; logging tapes.

Producer Projects—assist with news packages: viewing, researching and writing; assist photographers and producers on remotes; assist executive producer with daily and long term tasks.

Benefits
A statement from the educational institution verifying credit will be awarded upon successful completion of the program.

Contact
FOX Philadelphia
Andrea Previte
330 Market Street
Philadelphia, PA 19106

Phone: 215-925-2929 ext. 7155
Fax: 215-413-3832
URL: http://www.foxphiladelphia.com

WWLP TV22

General Information

In March of 1953 WWLP-TV began as a UHF TV station in Massachusetts.

Internships Available

Internships are scheduled year-round in the News, Engineering and Production/Promotion departments. *News Department*—interns in the newsroom gain industry experience handling many incoming and outgoing calls from the news desk. Interns learn the newsroom computer system and write and re-write stories from wire copy. Interns work closely with news producers on a daily basis.

Engineering Department—interns in the Engineering Department must be in school studying in the field of electronics. Interns work closely with engineers in the installation and maintenance of broadcast equipment. Send résumé and cover letter to dcote@wwlp.com.

Production/Promotion Department—interns in the Production/Promotion Department work closely with news, sales and programming departments to get newscasts, commercials and other local programming on the air. Work with directors, assistant directors, studio camera operators, audio booth operators, graphic artists, master control operators and announcers during live and taped programming.

Benefits

Non-paid internships. Students can receive course credits.

Contact
WWLP-TV22
PO Box 2210
Springfield, MA 01102-2210

Phone: 413-786-2200
E-mail: mgarreffi@wwlp.com for News Internship
dcote@wwlp.com for Engineering Internship
jbaran@wwlp.com for Production Internship
URL: http://www.wwlp.com

WXIN-TV

General Information
Partners of Tribune Company, a media company with operations in television and radio broadcasting, publishing, education and interactive ventures.

Internship Available
FOX 59 is looking for talented interns to assist and learn the methods of operation at the station. Successful candidates will learn the fundamentals of a fast-paced department while working with all facets of a broadcasting operation. WXIN has internship opportunities in the following departments: Promotion/Creative Services, Community Affairs, News, Operations/ Engineering. Interns may work between 20 - 40 hours a week depending on class schedule.

Benefits
Internships are non-compensated and for school credit only.

Contact
WXIN-TV
Internship Coordinator
1440 N. Meridian St.
Indianapolis, IN 46202

Phone: 317-632-5900
URL: http://www.wxin.com

Xerox Research & Technology

General Information

A high tech computer research facility that creates hardware and software programs.

Internships Available

Xerox Research & Technology offers summer opportunities in research and technology developments. Internship areas include: Algorithms, Computer Architecture & Digital Systems, Computer Science Theory, Computer Supported Cooperative Work, Computer Vision & Image, Understanding Digital Libraries, Distributed Systems, Electronic Materials, Graphics & Imaging, Image Analysis and Recognition, Linguistics, Materials Science, Mobile Computing Networking & Protocols, User Interfaces. Eligibility: Successful applicants typically hold Bachelor's degrees in Computer Science, Mathematics, Physics, Electrical Engineering, or related fields and are enrolled in advanced degree programs by the time internships begin. Graduates can be eligible for permanent employment opportunities. There are no residency requirements. Qualifications: Match students' with project requirements. The company reads letters of recommendation in an attempt to gain information about the applicant's accomplishments, work habits, creativity, and dedication. Preference for academically mature students who are likely to be productive during a 3-month internship. December 1 and February 15 deadline.

Benefits

Paid with opportunity for college credits.

Contact

Ms. Carleen Martin
Summer Internship
Xerox Research & Technology
3400 Hillview Avenue
Palo Alto, CA 94304

Phone: 650-813-7127
E-mail: interns@pal.xerox.com

Zooma Zooma

General Information

A bi-coastal production company specializing in commercials, music videos and short films. Established 8 years ago, Zooma Zooma's goal is to create an exciting production company for unique, young film makers to showcase talent.

Internships Available

College student or recent grad. Smart, learns quickly, and able to handle multiple tasks. Assist the Office Manager, Production Coordinator, and Producers. Must be good on the phone and have some knowledge of Word and other multimedia/design programs. Fast paced office. Learn about the film production industry.

Benefits

This is an unpaid internship, and there are no stipends, but college credits are awarded. If interested, fax résumés.

Contact

Susan Pickover
Production Coordinator
Zooma Zooma
11 Mercer Street, 3rd floor
New York, NY 10013
Phone: 212-941-7680
Fax: 212-941-8179

Zooma Zooma
804 Main St.
Suite 200
Venice, CA 90291
Phone: 310-392-8676
Fax: 310-392-0636

E-mail: susan@zoomazooma.com

Directories & Indices

International Festivals & Conference

3D Festival
October
Malmo, Sweden
http://www.3dfestival.com

Ajijic Film Festival
November
Guadalajara, Mexico
Phone: 011-52-376-6-0351
http://www.mexconnect.com"

Animac, Mostra Int'l de Cinema
d'Animacio
October
Lleida, Spain
Phone: 011-34-973-700-392

The Animated Castles
October 15-17
Rome, Italy
Phone: 011-39-6-939-1577

Animation Kobe Awards
November
Kobe, Japan
Phone: 011-81-6-6342-3165

ASIFA-Hollywood 27th Annual
Annie Awards
November
Glendale, CA USA
Phone: 818-842-8330
http://www.asifa-hollywood.org

BAFTA Interactive Entertainment
Awards
October
London, England
Phone: 011-44-171-734-0022
http://www.bafta.org

Broadcast India '99 Exhibtion and
Symposium
October 19-23
Mumbai, India
Phone: 011-91-22-215-1396

Cartoombria Int'l Animation Festival
December 2-5
Perugia, Italy
Phone: 011-39-075-572-6764

Chicago Int'l Children's Film
Festival
October
Chicago, IL USA
Phone: 773-281-9075
http://www.cicff.org

COMDEX Fall
November
Las Vegas, NV USA
http://www.comdex.com

Digital Content Creation and Exhibition
December
Long Beach
Phone: 714-513-8400
http://www.advanstar.com

Digital Video Conference & Exposition
October
Long Beach, CA USA
Phone: 415-278-5258
http://www.dvexpo.com

East Coast Video Show
October 5-7
Atlantic City, NJ USA
Phone: 203-882-1300
http://www.ecvshow.com

European Gathering of Young
Digital Creation
November
Valenciennes, France
Phone: 011-33-55-34-24-24

Expo Television & Radio
November
Bogota, Colombia
Phone: 954-457-5910
http://www.tdcevents.com

Fantoche
June 15
Zurich, Switzerland
Phone: 41-1-361-41-51
http://www.fantoche.ch

FlickerFest: 9th Int'l Short Film
Festival
January
Sydney
Phone: 011-2-9365-6877011-2-9365-6899

Int'l Animated Film Festival
November
Espinho, Portugal
Phone: 011-02-734-4611

Int'l Children's Film Festival
November
Hyderbad, India
Phone: 011-92-22-387-0875

Int'l Emmy Awards
November
New York City, NY USA
Phone: 212-489-6869

Int'l Independent Film Festival of Ourense
November
Ourense, Spain
Phone: 011-34-988-224-127

2nd Int'l Student Animation Festival
October
Ottawa, Canada
Phone: 613-232-8769

Japan Digital Animation Festival
October
Nagoya, Japan
Fax: 011-81-52-231-6767
http://www.jdaf.gr.jp/

Kids World
November
Beijing
Phone: 011-8610-687-48902

London Effects & Animation
Festival (LEAF)
November
London
Phone: 011-44-181-994-7354

London Int'l Advertising
Awards Festival
November
London
Phone: 212-681-8844
http://www.liaawards.com

MACWORLD Expo/San Francisco
January
San Francisco
Fax: 781-440-0362
http://www.macworld.com/expo
Annual Mill Valley Film Festival
October
Mill Valley, CA USA.
Phone: 415-383-5256
http://www.finc.org

MIPAsia
December
Singapore
Phone: 033-141-90-45-80
http://www.mipasia.com

MIPCOM Jr.
October
Cannes, France
Phone: 011-33-141-90-44-00
http://www.mipcom.com

MIPCOM
October
Cannes, France
Phone: 011-33-141-90-44-00
http://www.mipcom.com

Ohio Independent Film
Festival & Market
November
Cleveland, OH USA
Phone: 216-781-1755
http://www.ohiofilms.com

San Francisco Independent Film Festival
December
San Francisco, CA USA
Phone: 415-929-5038
http://www.sfiff.org

Annual Savannah Film and
Video Festival
November
Savannah, GA
http://www.scad.edu/filmfest

SIGGRAPH
Conference July
Travel
http://www.siggraph.org

Spike and Mikeís Sick and
Twisted Festival of Animation
Traveling
http://www.spikeandmike.com

Telluride IndieFest
December
Telluride, CO USA.
Phone: 970-728-2629

Ulisses Int'l Children's Film and
Television Festival
October
Lisbon, Portugal
Phone: 011-351-1-302-0330

Vancouver Effects and Animation Festival
July
Vancouver, Canada
http://www.veaf.com

Vermont International Film
Festival
October
Burlington, VT USA
Phone: 802-660-2600
http://www.vtiff.org

A Week With the Masters
November
Trivandrum, Kerala,
India
Phone: 818-502-3088 or
011-91-471-416-929

Annual Worldfest-Flagstaff Int'l
Film Festival
November
Flagstaff, AZ USA
Phone: 713-965-9955
http://www.worldfest.org

Animation & New Media Company Directory

East Coast

ADVANCED IMAGING INC.
350 Center St.
Wallingford, CT 06492.
Medical and technical animation simulation

AERIAL IMAGE VIDEO SERVICES
137 W. 19th St.
NY, NY 10011
Motion control animation

ALCO COMPUTER GRAPHICS
302 Carlton Terrace
Teaneck, NJ 07666
2-D & 3D computer animation

ALEXANDER, SAM PRODUCTIONS, INC.
311W. 43rd St., #205
New York, NY 10036.
Motion graphics, titles, special visual effects

ANIMAGINATION, LTD.
259 W. 30th St.
New York, NY 10001

ANIMATED, INC.
1600 Broadway #301
New York, NY 10001
Humorous animation

ANIMUS FILMS
2W. 47th St., #1209
New York, NY 10036
Animation, stop motion

ANIVISION LTD.
981 Walnut St.
Pittsburgh, PA 15234
Traditional cel, rubber puppets and nixed animation

APA STUDIOS
230 W. 10th St.
New York, NY 10014.
Animation, special affects, live action stop motion & motion control

ATLANTIC MOTION PICTURES
162 W. 21st St., 4th floor
New York, NY 10011
Motion control, graphics, special effects & mixed media

AVEKTA PRODUCTIONS
164 Madison Ave., 4th floor,
New York, NY 10016
Computer graphics for animation

BXB, INC.
532 La Guardia Pl., #2L
New York, NY 10012
Computer graphics for animation

BECKERMAN, HOWARD ANIMATION INC.
35-38 169th St.
Flushing, NY 11358
Cel animation

BLUE SKYIVIFX
1 South Rd.
Harrison, NY 10528
High-end computer animation

BOCA ENTERTAINMENT
9128 Villa Portofino Circle
Boca Raton, FL 33496

BRAND, SUSAN STUDIO
41 Union Square West
New York, NY 10003

BROADWAY VIDEO DESIGN
1619 Broadway
New York, NY 10019
2-D & 3-D computer animation, art
direction & production

CACIOPPO PRODUCTIONS DESIGN,
INC.
42 E 23rd St., 5th Floor
New York, NY 10010
Computer animation, 2-D & 3-D,
broadcast & corporate

CAESAR VIDEO GRAPHICS
137 E. 25th St., 2nd Floor
New York, NY 10010
Paintbox computer graphics for animation

CAGED BEAGLE PRODUCTIONS
24 Elizabeth St.
Port Chester, NY 10573
Cel & character animation

CHARLEX
2W. 45th St., 7th Floor
New York, NY 10036
Animatics and photomatics

COREY DESIGNS STUDIO INC.
27 Chestnut Oval
Orangeburg, NY 10967
Character animation

CREATIVE FORCE ASSOCIATES
41 Oakdene Ave.
Cliffside Park, NJ 07010
Computer animation

CREATIVE WAYS
305 E. 46th St.
New York, NY 10017
Computer animation

CURIOUS PICTURES
440 Lafayette St., 6th Floor
New York, NY 10003
2-D & 3-D animation, clay & traditional
cel animation, mixed media, stop motion

COMMUNICATIONS PLUS
102 Madison Ave.
New York, NY 10016
Animatics and Photomatics

COMP ART PLUS
49th w. 45TH St., 4th floor
New York, NY 10036
Animatics

CONTINUITY
62W. 45th St., 10th floor
New York, NY 10036

CREATIVE WAYS
305 E. 46th St.
New York, NY 10017
Animatics and photomatics

DARINO FILMS
222 Park Ave.
South NY, NY 10028
Computer animation, special effects, 2-D &
3-D & interactive video

DASILVA ANIMATION
311 E. 85th St.
New York, NY 10028
Character design & cel animation,
computer graphics, 3-D animations

DOROS MOTION INC.
40 W. 21st St.
New York, NY 10010
Computer & traditional animation

EASTERN OPTICAL EFX, INC.
321 W. 44th St., 4th Floor, East
New York, NY 10036
Cel animation, slide animation, motion
picture optical effects

EDITEL
222 E. 44th St.
New York, NY 10017
Paintbox & 3-D Wavefront

EMPIRE VIDEO, INC.
216E. 45th St., 11th Floor
New York, NY 10017
2-D & 3D computer animation

F-STOP STUDIO
231W. 29th St., #203
New York, NY 10001
Cel animation, motion graphics, feature
titles, photo projections, 2-D & 3-D
computer animation, music videos

FEIGENBAUM, BILL DESIGNS INC.
15 W.26th St., #1615
New York, NY 10010
3-D animation/live action integration, cel

4-FRONT VIDEO DESIGN, INC.
1500 Broadway 5th Floor
New York, NY 10036
3-D, 2-D graphics

GGC, INC. MB # 3745
Attn.: Gardner
4450 Rivanna Lane
Fairfax VA 22030-4441
Animation, publishing, web design

GATI, JOHN FILM EFFECT
04-56 83rd PL.
Middle Village, NY 11379
3-D, production animation children's
program

GT GROUP Division of Griffith &
Tekushan
630 9th Ave.
10001 NY, NY 10036
Paintbox, 2-D & 3-D computer animation

R/GREENBERG ASSOCIATES, INC.
350 W. 39th St.
New York, NY 10018

INDUSTRIAL LIGHT & MAGIC FILM
1 Union Square West #205
New York, NY 10003

THE INK TANK
2W. 47th St., 14th Floor
New York, NY 10036

JANOS, FRONZ PRODUCTIONS
104 Valley Rd.
Katonah, NY 10536
3-D animation & computer graphics for
TV

MANHATTAN TRANSFER
545 Fifth Ave., Fifth Fl.
New York, NY 10017
Digital effects

MTV ANIMATION
1515 Broadway 24th Fl.
New York, NY 10036

NAPOLEON VIDEOGRAPHICS
460 W. 42nd St.
New York, NY 10036
Animatics, photomatics, live action test

NATIONAL VIDEO INDUSTRIES, INC.
15W. 17th St.
New York, NY 10011
Video Animatics

ROSEBUSH COMPANY, JUDSON
154 W. 57th St., #826
New York, NY 10019-3321
Multimedia

STARGATE VIDEO, INC.
305 E. 47th St., Concourse level
New York, NY 10017
Animatics, live action

VIDEO STORYBOARD TESTS
107 E. 31st St., 5th floor
New York, NY 10016
Animatics, photomatics, and test
commercials

VIDEOWORKS POST AND & GRAPHICS
24W. 4Oth St.
New York, NY 10018

ZANDER ANIMATION PRODUCTION
118 E. 25th St.
New York, NY 10010
Cel and computer animation

ZERO DEGREES KELVIN
304 Hudson St.
New York, NY 10013
Computer animation

Mid-west

AHRENS CREATIVE GROUP INC.
400 N. State St.
Chicago, IL 60610.
Computer graphics, animation, audio, full
motion video

AMERICAN TIME LAPSE
3712 N. Broadway #282
Chicago, IL 60613
Time-lapse, stop action

ANIMATION STATION, LTD.
633 S. Plymouth Ct. #1103
Chicago, IL 60605.
Computer animation for broadcast and
video

AVID PRODUCTIONS, INC
372 W. Ontario #403
Chicago, IL 60610

CALABASH ANIMATION, INC.
657 W. Ohio St.
Chicago, IL 60610-3916
Traditional animation

THE CARTOON TYCOON
311
Harrisburg, PA 17120
Cel animation

CINEMA VIDEO CENTER
211 E. Grand Ave.
Chicago, IL 60611
2- & 3-D computer animation for video
application

CIONI ARTWORKS
1662 W. Hubbard St.
Chicago, IL 60610
Cel animation, character design & live
action animation compositing

CHARACTER BUILDERS, INC.
1476 Manning Pkwy
Powell, OH 43065
Animation & character design; design;
cleanups & layouts

West Coast

ANIMAGRAPHICS
206 N. Orehard Dr.
Burbank, CA 91506
Special effects; cel animation

CONTINUITY STUDIOS
4710 W. Magnolia Blvd.
Burbank, CA 91505
Animatics & Photomatics

D.J.N. STUDIOS INC.
16313 Clark Ave.
Bellflower, CA 90706
Animatics

ON TAPE PRODUCTIONS
724 Battery St., 2nd Floor
San Francisco, CA 94111
Animatics & Photomatics from 35mm
slides, color transfers, pin-registered
animation cels, photographs & flash art

PRO VIDEO
801 N. La Brea Ave., #104
Los Angeles, CA 90038
Animatics & Photomatics

ZONA PRODUCTIONS, INC.
215 S. La Cienega Blvd. #204
Beverly Hills, CA 90211
Videomatics-transferring slides & tape
with motion control; Paintbox

A.I.A. PRODUCTIONS
15132 La Maida St.
Sherman Oaks, CA 91403
Animatics & Graphics effects

ATV PRODUCTION CENTER
11367 Trade Center Dr., #105
Rancho Cordova, CA 95742
Broadcast graphics

ACCLAIM PRODUCTIONS
8691 Heil Ave.
Westminster, CA 92683
Macintosh, 2-D & 3-D

ACEVEDO, VICTOR
956 1/2 N. Vista St.
Los Angeles, CA 90046
3D animation

ACME FILMWORKS ANIMATION
6525 Sunset Blvd. #6
Hollywood, CA 90028
Animated commercial production; cel, clay,
model, 2-D & 3-D computer animation

ACTION VIDEO, INC.
6616 Lexington Ave.
Hollywood, CA 90028

ALLEN, DAVID PRODUCTIONS
918 W. Oak St.
Burbank, CA 91506
Visual effects, puppet animation

ANDERSON, HOWARD A. COMPANY
100 Universal City Plaza Bldg. 504 3rd
Floor
Universal City, CA 91608
Optical tiles & Special visual effects

ANGEL STUDIOS
5962 La Place Ct. #100
Carlsbad, CA 92008
3-D computer animation

ANIMAGRAPHICS
206 N. Orchard Dr.
Burbank, CA 91506
Rostriam photography, special effects, cel
animation, titles

ANIMATION RANCH
1720 Westinghouse St.
San Diego, CA 92111
Cartoon & graphic animation

AREA 17
1240 N. Hovenhurst Dr.
Los Angeles, CA 90046
Video performance, visual display, special
effects software & interactive presentation

ARTICHOKE PRODUCTIONS
4114 Linden St.
Oakland, CA 94608
Computer & Film animation

AVAILABLE LIGHT LTD.
3110 W. Burbank Blvd.
Burbank, CA 91505
Effects animation digital visual effects,
rotoscoping, including camera & optical
service

BAER ANIMATION COMPANY, INC
3765 Cahuenga Blvd.
West Studio City, CA 91604.
Classic cel animation

BECHTOLD STUDIOS
430 S. Niagara St.
Burbank, CA 91505
3-D animation, multimedia & video
games, computer animation, interactive
media

BLUM, DAVID ANIMATION
3733 Mound Vieto
Studio City, CA 91604
Computer graphics & special effects

BOYINGTON FILM PRODUCTIONS
5815 Blackwelder
Culver City, CA 90232
Stop-motion animation effects, live-action,
motion control computer-generated
graphics

BRANDLY NEON ANIMATION
120 S. Vignas St.,
Los Angeles, CA 90012

BRAVERMAN PRODUCTIONS, INC
10866 Wilshire Blvd. 10th Floor
Los Angeles, CA 90024
Kinestasis

BUBAR, LORRAINE
12748 Indianapolis St.,
Los Angeles, CA 90066
Motion graphics, cel animation

BUENA VISTA VISUAL EFFECTS
500 S Buena Vista St.
Burbank, CA 91521
Effects animation, matte painting & visual
effects, digital effects

CALIFORNIA COMMUNICATIONS INC
6900 Santa Monica Blvd.
Los Angeles, CA 90038
Computer graphics for broadcast

CALICO CREATIONS LTD
9340 Liton Ave.
Chaltsworth, CA 91311-5879
Computer & cel animation, motion-
control miniatures

CARLSON, LESLIE
2066 Paramount Dr.
Los Angeles, CA 90068
Computer animation

THE CHANDLER GROUP
4121 Redwood Ave.
Los Angeles CA 90066.
Motion control, rotoscoping & 35-70mm
3-D screen

CHEAP COMPUTER GRAPHICS
28938 Morningside Dr.
ValVerde, CA 91384
Computer animation

CHESSHER ANIMATION
18811 Napa St.
Northridge, CA 91324
Cel & special effects animation

CIMITYART
800 S Robertson Blvd. #9
Los Angeles, CA 90035

CINEMA ENGINEERING COMPANY
7243 Atoll Ave.
North Hollywood, CA 91605
Special visual effects

CINEMA RESEARCH
6860 Lexington Ave.
Los Angeles, CA 90038
Title design & special visual effects &
digital compositive

COLOSSAL PICTURES
2800 3rd St.
San Francisco, CA 94107
Animation & special effects

COMMUNICATION BRIDGES
180 Harbor Dr., #231
Sausalito, CA 94965
Full range from Macintosh to high-end &
animation graphics

COMPOSITE IMAGE SYSTEM/C.I.S.
1144 N. Las Palmas Ave.
Los Angeles, CA 90038
Special effects

COMPUTER CAFE
3130 Skyway Dr., #603
Santa Maria, CA 93455
2-D & 3-D animation

CONTINUITY STUDIOS
4710 w. Magnolia Blvd.
Burbank, CA 91505
3-D computer graphics for animation

CORNELL/ABOOD INC.
4121 1/2 Radford Ave.
Studio City, CA 91604
Animation & live action for commercial &
television

CREATIVE CONNECTIONS
INTERNATIONAL
500 Redondo Ave., #203
Long Beach, CA 90814
Animation design

CREATIVE ALLIANCE INC.
6523 1/2 Leland Way
Los Angeles, CA 90028
Computer animation

CRUSE & COMPANY
7000 Romaine St.
Los Angeles CA 90038
Opticals special effects

DIGITAL MAGIC
3000 W. Olympic Blvd., Bldg. 1
Santa Monica, CA 90404
D-1 animation, computer graphics &
compositing

DIGITAL FACADES
1140 Westwood Blvd., #201
Los Angeles, CA 90024
3-D modeling

DOURMASHKIN PRODUCTIONS
3852 Camino de Solona
Sherman Oaks, CA 91423
Cel animation, 3-D computer graphics,
stop-motion, clay animation, rotoscoping

DOWLEN, JAMES
P.O. Box 15152
Santa Rosa, CA 95402
Topas, frame by frame animation

DREAM QUEST IMAGES
2635 Park Center Dr.
Simi Valley, CA 93065
Animation, motion control, special effects
including matte painting & digital
DUCK SOUP PRODUCKIONS
2205 Stoner Ave.
Los Angeles, CA 90064
Animation/live action

DUDA DESIGN
16707 Sunset Blvd.
Pacific Palisades, CA 90272
Computer animation, optical special
effects, interactive multimedia

E.P. GRAPHICS PRODUCTION
2525 N. Naomi
Burbank, CA 91504
3-D animation

EFFECTS/GENE YOUNG
517 W. Windsor Rd.
Glendale, CA 91204
Special visual effects

ELECTRIC FILMWORKS
820 Thompson Ave #39
Glendale, CA 91201
Motion control, optical effects

FX + DESIGN
3025 W. Olympic Blvd.
Santa Monica, CA 90404
Graphics & special effects for TV & film

FILM ROMAN
12020 Chandler Blvd., #200
North Hollywood, CA 91607

FLINT PRODUCTIONS, INC.
1015 N. Orlando Ave.
Los Angeles, CA 90069
Special effects

FOX ANIMATION STUDIOS
2747 E. Camelback Rd.
Phoenix AZ 85016

GRFX/NOVOCOM
6314 Santa Monica Blvd.
Hollywood, CA 90038
Special effects, animation, title sequences,
graphic computer animation

GANG OF ART
2211 4th St., #204
Santa Monica, CA 90405
PC & Macintosh video, still graphic design
& production for interactive/multimedia

GENNIS, SARVANIMATRIX
2045 Holly Dr., #D
Hollywood, CA 90068
Effects, graphic & character animation

GEORGE & COMPANY
4044 E. Pacific St.
Highland, CA 92436
Animation, motion graphics

GRANT & MITCHELL
7835 Balboa Blvd.
Van Nuys, CA 91406
3-D animation

GRAEZ ENTERTAINMENT, INC.
1745 Victory Blvd.
Glendale, CA 91201

HANNA-BARBERA PRODUCTIONS,
INC.
3400 Cahuenga Blvd.
Los Angeles, CA 90068

HANSARD ENTERPRISES
P.O. Box 469
Culver City, CA 90232
Blue screen, front & rear projection

HAPPY TRAILS ANIMATION
3916 SW Huber St
Portland, OR 97219

HAYDOCK, BOB
49 Shelley Dr.
Mill Valley, CA 94941
Computer animation

HOMER & ASSOCIATES, INC
1420 N. Beachwood Dr.
Hollywood, CA 90028
3-D computer animation, special effects &
frame control

HOUSE FILM DESIGN
7033 W. Sunset Blvd., #301
Los Angeles, CA 90028
Animation & title design

HUERTA STUDIO
5225 Blackeslee Ave., #424
North Hollywood, CA 90028
Character & graphic animation including
layout, character design & storyboards

INTROVISION INTERNATIONAL
1011 N. Fuller Ave.
Los Angeles, CA 90046
Special effects & visual effects

JELLEY, CHRISTOPHER PRODUCTIONS
1040 1/2 N. Croft Ave.
Los Angeles, CA 90069
Special visual effects, animation
conceptualization, film design

KARZEN COMMUNICATION
6311 Romaine St., #7104
Los Angeles, CA 90038

KEESHEN, JIM PRODUCTIONS
1950 Saxotelle Blvd., #220
Los Angeles, CA 90025
Cel animation, character design, motion
control

KENIMATION ANIMATION SERVICES
1424 N. Wilcox Ave.
Hollywood, CA 90028
Titles, aerial images, montages, animation
camera

KLASKY CSUPO INC.
1258 N. Highland Ave.
Hollywood, CA 90038
Character animation, title sequencing, TV
programming

KLEISER-WALCZK CONSTRUCTION
COMPANY
6105 Mulholland Hwy.
Hollywood, CA 90068
Computer animation, digital character
creations, architectural & agricultural
database for animation & virtual reality

KROYER FILMS, INC.
12517 Chandler Blvd., #203
North Hollywood, CA 91607
Computer animation, commercials &
theatrical features, motion picture title
sequence

KURTZ & FRIENDS FILMS
2312 W. Olive Ave.
Burbank, CA 91506
Cel animation & special effects for
commercials, film titles

LSI GRAPHIC EVIDENCE
200 Corporate Pointe #300
Culver City, CA 90230

LANDMARK ENTERTAINMENT GROUP
5200 Lamkershin Blvd.
North Hollywood, CA 91601
Animation & special effects

LASER MEDIA, INC
6383 Arizona Circle
Los Angeles, CA 90045
Digital graphics

THE LEPREVOST CORP.
29350 Pacific Coast Hwy #6
Malibu, CA 90265
Film & broadcast animated title design

LUMENI PRODUCTIONS, INC
1632 Flower St.
Glendale, CA 91201
Computer animation, main & end titles,
motion graphics & special effects

MacLEOD PRODUCTIONS
2617 5th St., Santa Monica
CA 90405
Visual effects

MAGIC BOX PRODUCTIONS, INC.
345 N. Maple Dr., #222
Beverly Hills, CA 90210
Virtual reality & interactive media

MARKS COMMUNICATION, INC
2690 Beachwood Dr.
Los Angeles, CA 90068
Interactive media & graphic design

MARRS, LEE ARTWORK
1629 Parker St.
Berkeley, CA 94703
2D & 3D computer animation,
storyboards, Macintosh animation

THE MEDIA STAFF
6926 Melrose Ave.
Los Angeles, CA 90038
Aurora & Macintosh platforms

MELENDEZ, BILL PRODUCTIONS 439
N. Larchmont Blvd., LA, CA 90004

MERCER TITLES & OPTICAL EFFECTS,
LTD
106 W. Burbank Blvd.
Burbank, CA 91502
Optical special effects, titles

METROLIGHT STUDIOS
5724 W. 3rd St., #400
Los Angeles, CA 90036
3-D computer animation & special effects

MIDLAND PRODUCTION CORP.
435 S. 2nd St.
Richmond CA 94804. Visual film effects

MODERN VIDEOFILM
4411 W. Olive Ave.
Burbank CA 91505
Computer animation, visual effects &
motion control

MORALES, SUZANNE
4143 Hatfield Pl.
Los Angeles, CA 90032
Video & broadcast TV graphics, paintbox

MOTION CITY FILMS
1847 Centinela Ave.
Santa Monica CA 90404
Cel & computer animation, rotoscoping

MOTIONWORKS
953 N. Highland Ave.
Los Angeles CA 90038
Computer graphic animation

MULTIMEDIA PRODUCTIONS
PO Box 494155
Redding CA 96049-4155
2-D & 3-D animation special effects

NEW HOLLYWOOD INC
1302 N. Cahuenga Blvd.
Hollywood CA 90028.
Animation camera services, special effects,
titles, Cinemascope animation

PACIFIC DATA IMAGES
3101 Park Blvd.
Palo Alto CA 94306
Computer animation

PIXAR
1001 West Cutting
Richmond, CA 94804
Computer animation

WARNER BROS. TELEVISION &
CLASSIC ANIMATION
15305 Ventura Blvd., Suite 1200
Sherman Oaks, CA 91403

XAOS INC.
444 De Haro St.
San Francisco, CA 94107
Computer animation

List of Channels Allotted by The FCC for Digital Television

WJSUTV AL ANNISTON
WDBB   AL BESSEMER
WBRCTV AL BIRMINGHAM
WBIQ   AL BIRMINGHAM
WVTMTV AL BIRMINGHAM
WBMG   AL BIRMINGHAM
WABM   AL BIRMINGHAM
WIIQ   AL DEMOPOLIS
WTVY   AL DOTHAN
WDHN   AL DOTHAN
WDIQ   AL DOZIER
WOWLTV AL FLORENCE
WYLE   AL FLORENCE
WFIQ   AL FLORENCE
WNALTV AL GADSDEN
WTJP   AL GADSDEN
WTTO   AL HOMEWOOD
WHNTTV AL HUNTSVILLE
WHIQ   AL HUNTSVILLE
WAAYTV AL HUNTSVILLE
WAFF   AL HUNTSVILLE
WZDX   AL HUNTSVILLE
WGIQ   AL LOUISVILLE
WKRGTV AL MOBILE
WALATV AL MOBILE
WPMI   AL MOBILE
WMPVTV AL MOBILE
WEIQ   AL MOBILE
WSFA   AL MONTGOMERY
WCOVTV AL MONTGOMERY
WAIQ   AL MONTGOMERY
WHOATV AL MONTGOMERY
WMCFTV AL MONTGOMERY
WCIQ   AL MOUNT CHEAHA
WSWSTV AL OPELIKA
WDFXTV AL OZARK
WAKA   AL SELMA
WRJMTV AL TROY
WCFTTV AL TUSCALOOSA
NEW   AL TUSKEGEE
KETG   AR ARKADELPHIA
KTVE   AR EL DORADO
KAFT   AR FAYETTEVILLE
KHOGTV AR FAYETTEVILLE

KFSMTV AR FORT SMITH
KPOMTV AR FORT SMITH
KHBS AR FORT SMITH
KVTH AR HOT SPRINGS
KAITTV AR JONESBORO
KTEJ AR JONESBORO
KVTJ AR JONESBORO
KETS AR LITTLE ROCK
KARKTV AR LITTLE ROCK
KATV AR LITTLE ROCK
KTHV AR LITTLE ROCK
KLRT AR LITTLE ROCK
KVUT AR LITTLE ROCK
KEMV AR MOUNTAIN VIEW
KLEP AR NEWARK
KVTN AR PINE BLUFF
KASN AR PINE BLUFF
KFAA AR ROGERS
KSBNTV AR SPRINGDALE
KNAZTV AZ FLAGSTAFF
KTFL AZ FLAGSTAFF
KCFG AZ FLAGSTAFF
KKTM AZ FLAGSTAFF
KXGR AZ GREEN VALLEY
KMOHTV AZ KINGMAN
KMCC AZ LAKE HAVASU CIT
KPNX AZ MESA
KTVK AZ PHOENIX
KPHOTV AZ PHOENIX
KAET AZ PHOENIX
KSAZTV AZ PHOENIX
KNXVTV AZ PHOENIX
KPAZTV AZ PHOENIX
KTVWTV AZ PHOENIX
KUTPTV AZ PHOENIX
KASW AZ PHOENIX
KUSK AZ PRESCOTT
KAUC AZ SIERRA VISTA
KAJW AZ TOLLESON
KVOA AZ TUCSON
KUATTV AZ TUCSON
KGUN AZ TUCSON
KMSBTV AZ TUCSON
KOLDTV AZ TUCSON
KTTUTV AZ TUCSON
KUASTV AZ TUCSON
KHRR AZ TUCSON
KYMA AZ YUMA
KSWT AZ YUMA

KDOCTV CA ANAHEIM
KAEF CA ARCATA
KGET CA BAKERSFIELD
KEROTV CA BAKERSFIELD
KBAKTV CA BAKERSFIELD
KUZZTV CA BAKERSFIELD
KHIZ CA BARSTOW
KAJB CA CALIPATRIA
KBSV CA CERES
KHSLTV CA CHICO
KCPM CA CHICO
KGMC CA CLOVIS
KTNCTV CA CONCORD
KVEA CA CORONA
KRCB CA COTATI
KVYE CA EL CENTRO
KECYTV CA EL CENTRO
KIEMTV CA EUREKA
KVIQ CA EUREKA
KEET CA EUREKA
KBVU CA EUREKA
KFWU CA FORT BRAGG
KVPT CA FRESNO
KSEE CA FRESNO
KFSNTV CA FRESNO
KJEO CA FRESNO
KAIL CA FRESNO
KFTV CA HANFORD
KOCETV CA HUNTINGTON BEAC
KCBSTV CA LOS ANGELES
KNBC CA LOS ANGELES
KTLATV CA LOS ANGELES
KABCTV CA LOS ANGELES
KCALTV CA LOS ANGELES
KTTV CA LOS ANGELES
KCOPTV CA LOS ANGELES
KWHYTV CA LOS ANGELES
KCET CA LOS ANGELES
KMEXTV CA LOS ANGELES
KLCS CA LOS ANGELES
KNSO CA MERCED
KCSO CA MODESTO
KION CA MONTEREY
KSMSTV CA MONTEREY
KWOK CA NOVATO
KTVU CA OAKLAND
KHSCTV CA ONTARIO
KADYTV CA OXNARD
KMIRTV CA PALM SPRINGS

KESQTV CA PALM SPRINGS
KCVU   CA PARADISE
KKAG   CA PORTERVILLE
KRPA   CA RANCHO PALOS VE
KRCRTV CA REDDING
KIXETV CA REDDING
KRCA   CA RIVERSIDE
KCRATV CA SACRAMENTO
KVIE   CA SACRAMENTO
KXTV   CA SACRAMENTO
KCMY   CA SACRAMENTO
KPWBTV CA SACRAMENTO
KTXL   CA SACRAMENTO
KSBW   CA SALINAS
KCBA   CA SALINAS
KSCI   CA SAN BERNARDINO
KVCRTV CA SAN BERNARDINO
KZKI   CA SAN BERNARDINO
KFMBTV CA SAN DIEGO
KGTV   CA SAN DIEGO
KPBS   CA SAN DIEGO
KNSD   CA SAN DIEGO
KUSITV CA SAN DIEGO
KSWB   CA SAN DIEGO
KRONTV CA SAN FRANCISCO
KPIXTV CA SAN FRANCISCO
KGOTV   CA SAN FRANCISCO
KQED   CA SAN FRANCISCO
KDTV   CA SAN FRANCISCO
KOFYTV CA SAN FRANCISCO
KTSF   CA SAN FRANCISCO
KMTPTV CA SAN FRANCISCO
KCNS   CA SAN FRANCISCO
KBHKTV CA SAN FRANCISCO
KNTV   CA SAN JOSE
KICUTV CA SAN JOSE
KSTS   CA SAN JOSE
KTEH   CA SAN JOSE
KLXVTV CA SAN JOSE
KSBY   CA SAN LUIS OBISPO
KADE   CA SAN LUIS OBISPO
KCSMTV CA SAN MATEO
KMSGTV CA SANGER
KTBNTV CA SANTA ANA
KEYTTV CA SANTA BARBARA
NEW   CA SANTA BARBARA
KCOYTV CA SANTA MARIA
KFTY   CA SANTA ROSA
KOVR   CA STOCKTON

KQCA   CA STOCKTON
KFTL   CA STOCKTON
KVMD   CA TWENTYNINE PALM
KPSTTV CA VALLEJO
KSTVTV CA VENTURA
KMPH   CA VISALIA
KNXT   CA VISALIA
KCAH   CA WATSONVILLE
KTVJ   CO BOULDER
KBDITV CO BROOMFIELD
KWHD   CO CASTLE ROCK
KKTV   CO COLORADO SPRING
KRDOTV CO COLORADO SPRING
KXRMTV CO COLORADO SPRING
KWGNTV CO DENVER
KCNCTV CO DENVER
KRMATV CO DENVER
KMGHTV CO DENVER
KUSATV CO DENVER
KTVD   CO DENVER
KDVR   CO DENVER
KRMT   CO DENVER
KCEC   CO DENVER
KUBD   CO DENVER
KREZTV CO DURANGO
KFCT   CO FORT COLLINS
KREGTV CO GLENWOOD SPRING
KFQX   CO GRAND JUNCTION
KREXTV CO GRAND JUNCTION
KJCT   CO GRAND JUNCTION
KKCO   CO GRAND JUNCTION
KRMJ   CO GRAND JUNCTION
KDEN   CO LONGMONT
KREYTV CO MONTROSE
KOAATV CO PUEBLO
KTSC   CO PUEBLO
KSBSTV CO STEAMBOAT SPRIN
KTVS   CO STERLING
WHAITV CT BRIDGEPORT
WEDW   CT BRIDGEPORT
WFSB   CT HARTFORD
WHCTTV CT HARTFORD
WEDH   CT HARTFORD
WTICTV CT HARTFORD
WVIT   CT NEW BRITAIN
WTNH   CT NEW HAVEN
WBNE   CT NEW HAVEN
WEDY   CT NEW HAVEN
WTWS   CT NEW LONDON

WEDN	CT	NORWICH
WTXX	CT	WATERBURY
WRCTV	DC	WASHINGTON
WTTG	DC	WASHINGTON
WJLATV	DC	WASHINGTON
WUSA	DC	WASHINGTON
WDCA	DC	WASHINGTON
WETATV	DC	WASHINGTON
WHMM	DC	WASHINGTON
WBDCTV	DC	WASHINGTON
WDPB	DE	SEAFORD
WHYYTV	DE	WILMINGTON
WTGITV	DE	WILMINGTON
WPPBTV	FL	BOCA RATON
WFCT	FL	BRADENTON
WFTX	FL	CAPE CORAL
WCLF	FL	CLEARWATER
WKCF	FL	CLERMONT
WTGLTV	FL	COCOA
WBCC	FL	COCOA
WESH	FL	DAYTONA BEACH
WNTO	FL	DAYTONA BEACH
WSCV	FL	FORT LAUDERDALE
WINKTV	FL	FORT MYERS
WBBHTV	FL	FORT MYERS
WGCU	FL	FORT MYERS
WTCE	FL	FORT PIERCE
WTVX	FL	FORT PIERCE
WFGX	FL	FORT WALTON BEA
WPAN	FL	FORT WALTON BEA
WAWD	FL	FORT WALTON BEA
WUFT	FL	GAINESVILLE
WCJBTV	FL	GAINESVILLE
WGFL	FL	HIGH SPRINGS
WYHSTV	FL	HOLLYWOOD
WJXT	FL	JACKSONVILLE
WJCT	FL	JACKSONVILLE
WTLV	FL	JACKSONVILLE
WJWB	FL	JACKSONVILLE
WAWS	FL	JACKSONVILLE
WTEVTV	FL	JACKSONVILLE
WJEBTV	FL	JACKSONVILLE
WWFD	FL	KEY WEST
WEYS	FL	KEY WEST
WHBI	FL	LAKE WORTH
WWWB	FL	LAKELAND
WLCBTV	FL	LEESBURG
WACX	FL	LEESBURG
WFXU	FL	LIVE OAK
WBSF	FL	MELBOURNE
WIRB	FL	MELBOURNE
WPBT	FL	MIAMI
WFORTV	FL	MIAMI
WTVJ	FL	MIAMI
WSVN	FL	MIAMI
WPLG	FL	MIAMI
WLRN	FL	MIAMI
WLTV	FL	MIAMI
WBFSTV	FL	MIAMI
WCTD	FL	MIAMI
WDZL	FL	MIAMI
WHFT	FL	MIAMI
WZVNTV	FL	NAPLES
WTVK	FL	NAPLES
WCEU	FL	NEW SMYRNA BEAC
WOGX	FL	OCALA
WJXX	FL	ORANGE PARK
WCPXTV	FL	ORLANDO
WFTV	FL	ORLANDO
WMFETV	FL	ORLANDO
WZWY	FL	ORLANDO
WOFL	FL	ORLANDO
WRBW	FL	ORLANDO
WFGC	FL	PALM BEACH
WJHGTV	FL	PANAMA CITY
WMBB	FL	PANAMA CITY
WPGX	FL	PANAMA CITY
WFSG	FL	PANAMA CITY
WPCT	FL	PANAMA CITY BEA
WEARTV	FL	PENSACOLA
WSRE	FL	PENSACOLA
WHBR	FL	PENSACOLA
WJTC	FL	PENSACOLA
WWSB	FL	SARASOTA
WTSP	FL	ST PETERSBURG
WTTA	FL	ST. PETERSBURG
WTOG	FL	ST. PETERSBURG
WFSUTV	FL	TALLAHASSEE
WTXLTV	FL	TALLAHASSEE
WTWCTV	FL	TALLAHASSEE
WEDU	FL	TAMPA
WFLATV	FL	TAMPA
WTVT	FL	TAMPA
WUSFTV	FL	TAMPA
WFTS	FL	TAMPA
WBHSTV	FL	TAMPA
WPBF	FL	TEQUESTA
WRXYTV	FL	TICE

WBSVTV FL VENICE
WPTV   FL WEST PALM BEACH
WPEC   FL WEST PALM BEACH
WFLX   FL WEST PALM BEACH
WXELTV FL WEST PALM BEACH
WALBTV GA ALBANY
WFXL   GA ALBANY
WGTV   GA ATHENS
WNGMTV GA ATHENS
WSBTV GA ATLANTA
WAGATV GA ATLANTA
WXIATV GA ATLANTA
WTBS   GA ATLANTA
WPBA   GA ATLANTA
WATL   GA ATLANTA
WGNX   GA ATLANTA
WATC   GA ATLANTA
WUPA   GA ATLANTA
WJBF   GA AUGUSTA
WRDWTV GA AUGUSTA
WAGT   GA AUGUSTA
WFXG   GA AUGUSTA
WTLH   GA BAINBRIDGE
WUBI   GA BAXLEY
WBSGTV GA BRUNSWICK
WCLPTV GA CHATSWORTH
WDCOTV GA COCHRAN
WRBL   GA COLUMBUS
WTVM   GA COLUMBUS
WJSPTV GA COLUMBUS
WLTZ   GA COLUMBUS
WXTX   GA COLUMBUS
WSSTTV GA CORDELE
WELF   GA DALTON
WACSTV GA DAWSON
WMAZTV GA MACON
WGXA   GA MACON
WMGT   GA MACON
WGNM   GA MACON
WHSG   GA MONROE
WABWTV GA PELHAM
WPGATV GA PERRY
WTLKTV GA ROME
WSAVTV GA SAVANNAH
WVANTV GA SAVANNAH
WTOCTV GA SAVANNAH
WJCL   GA SAVANNAH
WCTV   GA THOMASVILLE
WNEGTV GA TOCCOA

WGVP   GA VALDOSTA
WXGATV GA WAYCROSS
WCESTV GA WRENS
WOITV IA AMES
KJMH   IA BURLINGTON
KGAN   IA CEDAR RAPIDS
KCRGTV IA CEDAR RAPIDS
KFXA   IA CEDAR RAPIDS
KTVC   IA CEDAR RAPIDS
KBINTV IA COUNCIL BLUFFS
KWQCTV IA DAVENPORT
KLJBTV IA DAVENPORT
KQCT   IA DAVENPORT
KCCI   IA DES MOINES
KDINTV IA DES MOINES
WHOTV IA DES MOINES
KDSMTV IA DES MOINES
KBTV   IA DES MOINES
KFXB   IA DUBUQUE
KTIN   IA FORT DODGE
KIINTV IA IOWA CITY
KWKB   IA IOWA CITY
KIMT   IA MASON CITY
KYIN   IA MASON CITY
KYOUTV IA OTTUMWA
KHIN   IA RED OAK
KTIV   IA SIOUX CITY
KCAUTV IA SIOUX CITY
KMEG   IA SIOUX CITY
KSINTV IA SIOUX CITY
NEW   IA SIOUX CITY
KWWL   IA WATERLOO
KRIN   IA WATERLOO
KBCITV ID BOISE
KAID   ID BOISE
KTVB   ID BOISE
KNINTV ID CALDWELL
KCDT   ID COEUR D'ALENE
KBGH   ID FILER
KIDK   ID IDAHO FALLS
KIFITV ID IDAHO FALLS
KLEWTV ID LEWISTON
KUIDTV ID MOSCOW
KIVI   ID NAMPA
KTRV   ID NAMPA
KPVI   ID POCATELLO
KISUTV ID POCATELLO
KMVT   ID TWIN FALLS
KIPT   ID TWIN FALLS

KXTF   ID TWIN FALLS
WEHSTV IL AURORA
WYZZTV IL BLOOMINGTON
WSIUTV IL CARBONDALE
WCIA   IL CHAMPAIGN
WICD   IL CHAMPAIGN
WEIUTV IL CHARLESTON
WBBMTV IL CHICAGO
WMAQTV IL CHICAGO
WLSTV IL CHICAGO
WGNTV IL CHICAGO
WTTW IL CHICAGO
WYCC IL CHICAGO
WCIUTV IL CHICAGO
WFLD IL CHICAGO
WCFCTV IL CHICAGO
WSNS IL CHICAGO
WAND IL DECATUR
WFHL IL DECATUR
WHSL IL EAST ST. LOUIS
WIFR IL FREEPORT
WSILTV IL HARRISBURG
WSEC IL JACKSONVILLE
WGBOTV IL JOLIET
WWTOTV IL LASALLE
WMEC IL MACOMB
WTCT IL MARION
WQADTV IL MOLINE
WQPTTV IL MOLINE
WCEE IL MOUNT VERNON
WUSITV IL OLNEY
WHOI IL PEORIA
WEEKTV IL PEORIA
WMBDTV IL PEORIA
WTVP IL PEORIA
WAOE IL PEORIA
WGEMTV IL QUINCY
WTJR IL QUINCY
WQEC IL QUINCY
WHBFTV IL ROCK ISLAND
WREXTV IL ROCKFORD
WTVO IL ROCKFORD
WQRFTV IL ROCKFORD
WICS IL SPRINGFIELD
WCFN IL SPRINGFIELD
WRSPTV IL SPRINGFIELD
WILLTV IL URBANA
WCCU IL URBANA
WINM IN ANGOLA

WTTV   IN BLOOMINGTON
WTIU   IN BLOOMINGTON
WCLJ   IN BLOOMINGTON
WIIB   IN BLOOMINGTON
WSJV   IN ELKHART
WTVW   IN EVANSVILLE
WNIN   IN EVANSVILLE
WFIETV IN EVANSVILLE
WEHT   IN EVANSVILLE
WEVV   IN EVANSVILLE
WANETV IN FORT WAYNE
WPTA   IN FORT WAYNE
WKJGTV IN FORT WAYNE
WFWA   IN FORT WAYNE
WFFTTV IN FORT WAYNE
WPWRTV IN GARY
WYIN   IN GARY
WJYS   IN HAMMOND
WRTV   IN INDIANAPOLIS
WISHTV IN INDIANAPOLIS
WTHR   IN INDIANAPOLIS
WFYI   IN INDIANAPOLIS
WHMBTV IN INDIANAPOLIS
WXIN   IN INDIANAPOLIS
WTBU   IN INDIANAPOLIS
WTTK   IN KOKOMO
WLFITV IN LAFAYETTE
WNDYTV IN MARION
WIPB   IN MUNCIE
WKOI   IN RICHMOND
WFTE   IN SALEM
WNDUTV IN SOUTH BEND
WSBTTV IN SOUTH BEND
WNIT   IN SOUTH BEND
WHMETV IN SOUTH BEND
WTWO   IN TERRE HAUTE
WTHITV IN TERRE HAUTE
WBAKTV IN TERRE HAUTE
WVUT   IN VINCENNES
KLBY   KS COLBY
KBSDTV KS ENSIGN
KKFT   KS FORT SCOTT
KSNG   KS GARDEN CITY
KUPKTV KS GARDEN CITY
KBSLTV KS GOODLAND
KSNC   KS GREAT BEND
KBSHTV KS HAYS
KOOD   KS HAYS
KPTS   KS HUTCHINSON

KWCHTV KS HUTCHINSON
NEW   KS HUTCHINSON
KSWK   KS LAKIN
KMCI   KS LAWRENCE
KOAMTV KS PITTSBURG
KAASTV KS SALINA
KTWU   KS TOPEKA
WIBWTV KS TOPEKA
KSNT   KS TOPEKA
KTKATV KS TOPEKA
KSNW   KS WICHITA
KAKETV KS WICHITA
KSASTV KS WICHITA
KWCV   KS WICHITA
WKAS   KY ASHLAND
WTSF   KY ASHLAND
WLJC   KY BEATTYVILLE
WBKO   KY BOWLING GREEN
WKYUTV KY BOWLING GREEN
WKNT   KY BOWLING GREEN
WKGBTV KY BOWLING GREEN
WGRB   KY CAMPBELLSVILLE
WCVNTV KY COVINGTON
WDKYTV KY DANVILLE
WKZTTV KY ELIZABETHTOWN
WAGV   KY HARLAN
WKHA   KY HAZARD
WYMTTV KY HAZARD
WLEXTV KY LEXINGTON
WKYTTV KY LEXINGTON
WTVQTV KY LEXINGTON
WKLE   KY LEXINGTON
WAVE   KY LOUISVILLE
WHASTV KY LOUISVILLE
WKPCTV KY LOUISVILLE
WBNA   KY LOUISVILLE
WLKY   KY LOUISVILLE
WDRBTV KY LOUISVILLE
WKMJTV KY LOUISVILLE
WLCN   KY MADISONVILLE
WKMATV KY MADISONVILLE
WKMR   KY MOREHEAD
WAOM   KY MOREHEAD
WKMU   KY MURRAY
WXIXTV KY NEWPORT
WKOH   KY OWENSBORO
WKON   KY OWENTON
WPSDTV KY PADUCAH
WKPD   KY PADUCAH

WDKA   KY PADUCAH
WKPITV KY PIKEVILLE
WKSOTV KY SOMERSET
KALBTV LA ALEXANDRIA
KLPATV LA ALEXANDRIA
KLAXTV LA ALEXANDRIA
WBRZ   LA BATON ROUGE
WAFB   LA BATON ROUGE
WLPBTV LA BATON ROUGE
WVLA   LA BATON ROUGE
WGMB   LA BATON ROUGE
KAQY   LA COLUMBIA
KATC   LA LAFAYETTE
KLFYTV LA LAFAYETTE
KADN   LA LAFAYETTE
KLPBTV LA LAFAYETTE
KPLCTV LA LAKE CHARLES
KLTLTV LA LAKE CHARLES
KVHP   LA LAKE CHARLES
KNOETV LA MONROE
KLTMTV LA MONROE
WWLTV   LA NEW ORLEANS
WDSU   LA NEW ORLEANS
WVUE   LA NEW ORLEANS
WYESTV LA NEW ORLEANS
WHNO   LA NEW ORLEANS
WGNO   LA NEW ORLEANS
WLAETV LA NEW ORLEANS
WNOLTV LA NEW ORLEANS
WCCL   LA NEW ORLEANS
KTBSTV LA SHREVEPORT
KSLATV LA SHREVEPORT
KLTSTV LA SHREVEPORT
KMSSTV LA SHREVEPORT
KSHV   LA SHREVEPORT
WUPL   LA SLIDELL
KARD   LA WEST MONROE
KMCTTV LA WEST MONROE
WCDCTV MA ADAMS
WGBHTV MA BOSTON
WBZTV   MA BOSTON
WCVBTV MA BOSTON
WHDHTV MA BOSTON
WFXT   MA BOSTON
WSBKTV MA BOSTON
WGBXTV MA BOSTON
WABU   MA BOSTON
WLVITV MA CAMBRIDGE
WMFP   MA LAWRENCE

WHSHTV	MA MARLBOROUGH	
WLNETV	MA NEW BEDFORD	
WLWC	MA NEW BEDFORD	
WHRC	MA NORWELL	
WWLP	MA SPRINGFIELD	
WGGBTV	MA SPRINGFIELD	
WGBYTV	MA SPRINGFIELD	
WZBU	MA VINEYARD HAVEN	
WUNI	MA WORCESTER	
WYDN	MA WORCESTER	
WMPT	MD ANNAPOLIS	
WMARTV	MD BALTIMORE	
WBALTV	MD BALTIMORE	
WJZTV	MD BALTIMORE	
WHSWTV	MD BALTIMORE	
WBFF	MD BALTIMORE	
WNUVTV	MD BALTIMORE	
WMPB	MD BALTIMORE	
WFPT	MD FREDERICK	
WHAGTV	MD HAGERSTOWN	
WWPB	MD HAGERSTOWN	
WJAL	MD HAGERSTOWN	
WGPT	MD OAKLAND	
WBOCTV	MD SALISBURY	
WCPB	MD SALISBURY	
WMDT	MD SALISBURY	
WCBB	ME AUGUSTA	
WLBZ	ME BANGOR	
WABITV	ME BANGOR	
WVIITV	ME BANGOR	
WMEATV	ME BIDDEFORD	
WMEDTV	ME CALAIS	
WWLA	ME LEWISTON	
WMEBTV	ME ORONO	
WMTWTV	ME POLAND SPRING	
WCSH	ME PORTLAND	
WGMETV	ME PORTLAND	
WPXT	ME PORTLAND	
WAGMTV	ME PRESQUE ISLE	
WMEMTV	ME PRESQUE ISLE	
WCML	MI ALPENA	
WBKBTV	MI ALPENA	
WBSX	MI ANN ARBOR	
WUCXTV	MI BAD AXE	
WOTV	MI BATTLE CREEK	
WJUE	MI BATTLE CREEK	
WNEMTV	MI BAY CITY	
WWTV	MI CADILLAC	
WCMV	MI CADILLAC	

WGKI	MI CADILLAC
WBKP	MI CALUMET
WTOMTV	MI CHEBOYGAN
WJBKTV	MI DETROIT
WDIV	MI DETROIT
WXYZTV	MI DETROIT
WXON	MI DETROIT
WKBD	MI DETROIT
WTVS	MI DETROIT
WWJTV	MI DETROIT
WKARTV	MI EAST LANSING
WJMNTV	MI ESCANABA
WJRTTV	MI FLINT
WFUM	MI FLINT
WSMH	MI FLINT
WOOD	MI GRAND RAPIDS
WZZMTV	MI GRAND RAPIDS
WXMI	MI GRAND RAPIDS
WGVUTV	MI GRAND RAPIDS
WDHS	MI IRON MOUNTAIN
WHTV	MI JACKSON
WWMT	MI KALAMAZOO
WGVK	MI KALAMAZOO
WLLA	MI KALAMAZOO
WLNSTV	MI LANSING
WSYMTV	MI LANSING
WLAJ	MI LANSING
WCMW	MI MANISTEE
WLUC	MI MARQUETTE
WNMU	MI MARQUETTE
WADL	MI MOUNT CLEMENS
WCMUTV	MI MOUNT PLEASANT
WTLJ	MI MUSKEGON
WILXTV	MI ONONDAGA
WEYITV	MI SAGINAW
WAQP	MI SAGINAW
WGTQ	MI SAULT STE. MARI
WWUPTV	MI SAULT STE. MARI
WPBNTV	MI TRAVERSE CITY
WGTU	MI TRAVERSE CITY
WUCMTV	MI UNIVERSITY CENT
WGKU	MI VANDERBILT
KCCOTV	MN ALEXANDRIA
KSAX	MN ALEXANDRIA
KWCMTV	MN APPLETON
KAAL	MN AUSTIN
KSMQTV	MN AUSTIN
KAWE	MN BEMIDJI
KAWB	MN BRAINERD

KDLH   MN DULUTH
WDSETV MN DULUTH
WDIOTV MN DULUTH
KNLD   MN DULUTH
WIRT   MN HIBBING
KEYCTV MN MANKATO
WCCOTV MN MINNEAPOLIS
KMSPTV MN MINNEAPOLIS
KARE   MN MINNEAPOLIS
KLGTTV MN MINNEAPOLIS
WFTC   MN MINNEAPOLIS
KVBMTV MN MINNEAPOLIS
KRWF   MN REDWOOD FALLS
KTTC   MN ROCHESTER
KXLTTV MN ROCHESTER
KXLI   MN ST. CLOUD
KTCATV MN ST. PAUL
KSTPTV MN ST. PAUL
KTCITV MN ST. PAUL
KBRR   MN THIEF RIVER FAL
KCCWTV MN WALKER
KSMN   MN WORTHINGTON
KFVSTV MO CAPE GIRARDEAU
KBSI   MO CAPE GIRARDEAU
KOMUTV MO COLUMBIA
KMIZ   MO COLUMBIA
KHQATV MO HANNIBAL
KRCG   MO JEFFERSON CITY
KNLJ   MO JEFFERSON CITY
KODETV MO JOPLIN
KSNF   MO JOPLIN
KOZJ   MO JOPLIN
WDAFTV MO KANSAS CITY
KCTV   MO KANSAS CITY
KMBCTV MO KANSAS CITY
KCPT   MO KANSAS CITY
KCWB   MO KANSAS CITY
KSHBTV MO KANSAS CITY
KYFC   MO KANSAS CITY
KSMOTV MO KANSAS CITY
KTVO   MO KIRKSVILLE
KPOBTV MO POPLAR BLUFF
KMOSTV MO SEDALIA
KYTV   MO SPRINGFIELD
KOLR   MO SPRINGFIELD
KOZK   MO SPRINGFIELD
KDEBTV MO SPRINGFIELD
KSPR   MO SPRINGFIELD
KQTV   MO ST. JOSEPH

KTAJ   MO ST. JOSEPH
KTVITV MO ST. LOUIS
KMOV   MO ST. LOUIS
KSDK   MO ST. LOUIS
KETC   MO ST. LOUIS
KPLRTV MO ST. LOUIS
KNLC   MO ST. LOUIS
KDNLTV MO ST. LOUIS
WLOXTV MS BILOXI
WMAHTV MS BILOXI
WMAETV MS BOONEVILLE
WMAUTV MS BUDE
WCBITV MS COLUMBUS
WXVT   MS GREENVILLE
WABGTV MS GREENWOOD
WMAOTV MS GREENWOOD
WXXVTV MS GULFPORT
WHLT   MS HATTIESBURG
WBUY   MS HOLLY SPRINGS
WLBTTV MS JACKSON
WJTV   MS JACKSON
WAPT   MS JACKSON
WMPNTV MS JACKSON
WDBD   MS JACKSON
WDAMTV MS LAUREL
WTOKTV MS MERIDIAN
WMAWTV MS MERIDIAN
WMDN   MS MERIDIAN
WGBC   MS MERIDIAN
WMABTV MS MISSISSIPPI STA
WNTZ   MS NATCHEZ
WMAVTV MS OXFORD
WTVA   MS TUPELO
WLOVTV MS WEST POINT
KTVQ   MT BILLINGS
KSVI   MT BILLINGS
KULRTV MT BILLINGS
KCTZ   MT BOZEMAN
KUSM   MT BOZEMAN
KXLFTV MT BUTTE
KTVM   MT BUTTE
KWYB   MT BUTTE
KXGNTV MT GLENDIVE
KRTV   MT GREAT FALLS
KFBBTV MT GREAT FALLS
KTGF   MT GREAT FALLS
KHMT   MT HARDIN
KAQR   MT HELENA
KTVH   MT HELENA

KCFWTV	MT KALISPELL	WSFXTV	NC WILMINGTON
KYUSTV	MT MILES CITY	WUNJTV	NC WILMINGTON
KPAXTV	MT MISSOULA	WRAYTV	NC WILSON
KUFMTV	MT MISSOULA	WXII	NC WINSTON-SALEM
KECITV	MT MISSOULA	WUNLTV	NC WINSTON-SALEM
KTMF	MT MISSOULA	WXLVTV	NC WINSTON-SALEM
WLOS	NC ASHEVILLE	KBME	ND BISMARCK
WHNS	NC ASHEVILLE	KFYRTV	ND BISMARCK
WUNFTV	NC ASHEVILLE	KXMBTV	ND BISMARCK
WASVTV	NC ASHEVILLE	KBMY	ND BISMARCK
WJZY	NC BELMONT	WDAZTV	ND DEVILS LAKE
WAAP	NC BURLINGTON	KXMATV	ND DICKINSON
WUNCTV	NC CHAPEL HILL	KQCDTV	ND DICKINSON
WBTV	NC CHARLOTTE	KDSE	ND DICKINSON
WSOCTV	NC CHARLOTTE	KJRE	ND ELLENDALE
WCCB	NC CHARLOTTE	WDAYTV	ND FARGO
WCNCTV	NC CHARLOTTE	KVLYTV	ND FARGO
WTVI	NC CHARLOTTE	KFME	ND FARGO
WUNDTV	NC COLUMBIA	KVRR	ND FARGO
WUNGTV	NC CONCORD	KGFE	ND GRAND FORKS
WTVD	NC DURHAM	KJRR	ND JAMESTOWN
WRDC	NC DURHAM	KSRE	ND MINOT
WKFT	NC FAYETTEVILLE	KMOT	ND MINOT
WFAY	NC FAYETTEVILLE	KXMCTV	ND MINOT
WNCN	NC GOLDSBORO	KMCY	ND MINOT
WFMYTV	NC GREENSBORO	KNRR	ND PEMBINA
WUPNTV	NC GREENSBORO	KXJBTV	ND VALLEY CITY
WLXITV	NC GREENSBORO	KWSE	ND WILLISTON
WNCTTV	NC GREENVILLE	KUMVTV	ND WILLISTON
WYDO	NC GREENVILLE	KXMDTV	ND WILLISTON
WUNKTV	NC GREENVILLE	KLKE	NE ALBION
WHKYTV	NC HICKORY	KTNETV	NE ALLIANCE
WGHPTV	NC HIGH POINT	KMNETV	NE BASSETT
WUNMTV	NC JACKSONVILLE	KGIN	NE GRAND ISLAND
WFXZTV	NC JACKSONVILLE	KTVG	NE GRAND ISLAND
WAXN	NC KANNAPOLIS	KHASTV	NE HASTINGS
WBFX	NC LEXINGTON	KHNETV	NE HASTINGS
WUNETV	NC LINVILLE	KWNBTV	NE HAYES CENTER
WUNU	NC LUMBERTON	KHGITV	NE KEARNEY
WFXI	NC MOREHEAD CITY	KLNETV	NE LEXINGTON
WCTI	NC NEW BERN	KLKN	NE LINCOLN
WRALTV	NC RALEIGH	KOLN	NE LINCOLN
WLFL	NC RALEIGH	KUONTV	NE LINCOLN
WRAZ	NC RALEIGH	KSNK	NE MCCOOK
WUNPTV	NC ROANOKE RAPIDS	KRNETV	NE MERRIMAN
WRMY	NC ROCKY MOUNT	KXNETV	NE NORFOLK
WITNTV	NC WASHINGTON	KNOPTV	NE NORTH PLATTE
WWAY	NC WILMINGTON	KPNETV	NE NORTH PLATTE
WECT	NC WILMINGTON	KMTV	NE OMAHA

WOWT	NE	OMAHA
KETV	NE	OMAHA
KXVO	NE	OMAHA
KYNETV	NE	OMAHA
KPTM	NE	OMAHA
KDUHTV	NE	SCOTTSBLUFF
KSTF	NE	SCOTTSBLUFF
KSNBTV	NE	SUPERIOR
WEDBTV	NH	BERLIN
WNBU	NH	CONCORD
WNDS	NH	DERRY
WENHTV	NH	DURHAM
WEKWTV	NH	KEENE
WLEDTV	NH	LITTLETON
WMURTV	NH	MANCHESTER
WGOT	NH	MERRIMACK
WWACTV	NJ	ATLANTIC CITY
WACITV	NJ	ATLANTIC CITY
WGTW	NJ	BURLINGTON
WNJS	NJ	CAMDEN
WNJU	NJ	LINDEN
WNJN	NJ	MONTCLAIR
WNJB	NJ	NEW BRUNSWICK
WNET	NJ	NEWARK
WHSETV	NJ	NEWARK
WMBCTV	NJ	NEWTON
WXTV	NJ	PATERSON
WWORTV	NJ	SECAUCUS
WNJT	NJ	TRENTON
WHSPTV	NJ	VINELAND
WFMETV	NJ	WEST MILFORD
WMGMTV	NJ	WILDWOOD
KOBTV	NM	ALBUQUERQUE
KNMETV	NM	ALBUQUERQUE
KOATTV	NM	ALBUQUERQUE
KRQE	NM	ALBUQUERQUE
KNAT	NM	ALBUQUERQUE
KAZQ	NM	ALBUQUERQUE
KLUZTV	NM	ALBUQUERQUE
KASYTV	NM	ALBUQUERQUE
KOCT	NM	CARLSBAD
KVIHTV	NM	CLOVIS
KOFT	NM	FARMINGTON
KOBF	NM	FARMINGTON
KHFT	NM	HOBBS
KRWGTV	NM	LAS CRUCES
KZIA	NM	LAS CRUCES
KENW	NM	PORTALES
KOBR	NM	ROSWELL
KBIMTV	NM	ROSWELL
KRPV	NM	ROSWELL
KASATV	NM	SANTA FE
KCHF	NM	SANTA FE
NEW	NM	SANTA FE
KOVT	NM	SILVER CITY
KENV	NV	ELKO
KVVUTV	NV	HENDERSON
KVBC	NV	LAS VEGAS
KLASTV	NV	LAS VEGAS
KLVX	NV	LAS VEGAS
KTNV	NV	LAS VEGAS
KINC	NV	LAS VEGAS
KUPN	NV	LAS VEGAS
KFBT	NV	LAS VEGAS
KBLR	NV	PARADISE
KTVN	NV	RENO
KRNV	NV	RENO
KNPB	NV	RENO
KOLOTV	NV	RENO
KRXI	NV	RENO
KAMETV	NV	RENO
KRENTV	NV	RENO
KWNV	NV	WINNEMUCCA
WTEN	NY	ALBANY
WNYT	NY	ALBANY
WXXATV	NY	ALBANY
WOCD	NY	AMSTERDAM
WAQF	NY	BATAVIA
WBNGTV	NY	BINGHAMTON
WMGCTV	NY	BINGHAMTON
WICZTV	NY	BINGHAMTON
WSKGTV	NY	BINGHAMTON
WGRZTV	NY	BUFFALO
WIVBTV	NY	BUFFALO
WKBWTV	NY	BUFFALO
WNEDTV	NY	BUFFALO
WNEQTV	NY	BUFFALO
WUTV	NY	BUFFALO
WNYOTV	NY	BUFFALO
WWNYTV	NY	CARTHAGE
WYDC	NY	CORNING
WETMTV	NY	ELMIRA
WENYTV	NY	ELMIRA
WLIW	NY	GARDEN CITY
WNYB	NY	JAMESTOWN
WRNNTV	NY	KINGSTON
WCBSTV	NY	NEW YORK
WNBC	NY	NEW YORK

WNYW NY NEW YORK	WVIZ OH CLEVELAND
WABCTV NY NEW YORK	WQHSTV OH CLEVELAND
WPIX NY NEW YORK	WCMHTV OH COLUMBUS
WNYETV NY NEW YORK	WSYX OH COLUMBUS
WBISTV NY NEW YORK	WBNSTV OH COLUMBUS
WPTZ NY NORTH POLE	WTTE OH COLUMBUS
WNPITV NY NORWOOD	WOSUTV OH COLUMBUS
WCFETV NY PLATTSBURGH	WDTN OH DAYTON
WTBY NY POUGHKEEPSIE	WHIOTV OH DAYTON
WLNY NY RIVERHEAD	WPTD OH DAYTON
WROCTV NY ROCHESTER	WKEF OH DAYTON
WHECTV NY ROCHESTER	WRGTTV OH DAYTON
WOKR NY ROCHESTER	WLIO OH LIMA
WXXITV NY ROCHESTER	WTLW OH LIMA
WUHF NY ROCHESTER	WUAB OH LORAIN
WRGB NY SCHENECTADY	WMFDTV OH MANSFIELD
WMHT NY SCHENECTADY	WSFJTV OH NEWARK
WMHQ NY SCHENECTADY	WPTO OH OXFORD
WHSITV NY SMITHTOWN	WUXA OH PORTSMOUTH
WNGS NY SPRINGVILLE	WPBOTV OH PORTSMOUTH
WSTMTV NY SYRACUSE	WGGNTV OH SANDUSKY
WTVH NY SYRACUSE	WOIO OH SHAKER HEIGHTS
WIXT NY SYRACUSE	WTJC OH SPRINGFIELD
WCNYTV NY SYRACUSE	WTOVTV OH STEUBENVILLE
WNYSTV NY SYRACUSE	WTOLTV OH TOLEDO
WSYT NY SYRACUSE	WTVG OH TOLEDO
WKTV NY UTICA	WNWOTV OH TOLEDO
WUTR NY UTICA	WGTETV OH TOLEDO
WFXV NY UTICA	WUPW OH TOLEDO
WNPETV NY WATERTOWN	WLMB OH TOLEDO
WWTI NY WATERTOWN	WFMJTV OH YOUNGSTOWN
WAKCTV OH AKRON	WKBNTV OH YOUNGSTOWN
WEAO OH AKRON	WYTV OH YOUNGSTOWN
WBNXTV OH AKRON	WHIZTV OH ZANESVILLE
WNEO OH ALLIANCE	KTEN OK ADA
WOUBTV OH ATHENS	KDOR OK BARTLESVILLE
WBGUTV OH BOWLING GREEN	KWET OK CHEYENNE
WOUCTV OH CAMBRIDGE	KRSCTV OK CLAREMORE
WDLI OH CANTON	KAFU OK ENID
WOAC OH CANTON	KOET OK EUFAULA
WWHO OH CHILLICOTHE	KSWOTV OK LAWTON
WLWT OH CINCINNATI	KFORTV OK OKLAHOMA CITY
WCPOTV OH CINCINNATI	KOCOTV OK OKLAHOMA CITY
WKRCTV OH CINCINNATI	KWTV OK OKLAHOMA CITY
WCET OH CINCINNATI	KETA OK OKLAHOMA CITY
WSTRTV OH CINCINNATI	KTBOTV OK OKLAHOMA CITY
WKYCTV OH CLEVELAND	KOKHTV OK OKLAHOMA CITY
WEWSTV OH CLEVELAND	KOCB OK OKLAHOMA CITY
WJWTV OH CLEVELAND	KTLC OK OKLAHOMA CITY

KSBI   OK OKLAHOMA CITY
KMNZ   OK OKLAHOMA CITY
KGLBTV OK OKMULGEE
KAQS   OK SHAWNEE
KJRH   OK TULSA
KOTV   OK TULSA
KTUL   OK TULSA
KOEDTV OK TULSA
KOKITV OK TULSA
KTFO   OK TULSA
KWHB   OK TULSA
KWMJ   OK TULSA
KOABTV OR BEND
KTVZ   OR BEND
KCBYTV OR COOS BAY
KMTZ   OR COOS BAY
KOACTV OR CORVALLIS
KEZI   OR EUGENE
KVALTV OR EUGENE
KMTR   OR EUGENE
KEPB   OR EUGENE
KEVU   OR EUGENE
KOTI   OR KLAMATH FALLS
KFTS   OR KLAMATH FALLS
KDKF   OR KLAMATH FALLS
KTVR   OR LA GRANDE
KOBI   OR MEDFORD
KSYS   OR MEDFORD
KTVL   OR MEDFORD
KDRV   OR MEDFORD
KMVU   OR MEDFORD
NEW   OR PENDLETON
KATU   OR PORTLAND
KOIN   OR PORTLAND
KGW   OR PORTLAND
KOPBTV OR PORTLAND
KPTV   OR PORTLAND
KNMT   OR PORTLAND
KPIC   OR ROSEBURG
KROZ   OR ROSEBURG
KMTXTV OR ROSEBURG
KBSPTV OR SALEM
KWBP   OR SALEM
WLVTTV PA ALLENTOWN
WFMZTV PA ALLENTOWN
WTAJTV PA ALTOONA
WATMTV PA ALTOONA
WKBSTV PA ALTOONA
WBPHTV PA BETHLEHEM

WPSXTV PA CLEARFIELD
WICUTV PA ERIE
WJETTV PA ERIE
WSEE   PA ERIE
WQLN   PA ERIE
WFXP   PA ERIE
WPCBTV PA GREENSBURG
WHPTV PA HARRISBURG
WHTMTV PA HARRISBURG
WITFTV PA HARRISBURG
WWLF   PA HAZLETON
WJACTV PA JOHNSTOWN
WWCPTV PA JOHNSTOWN
WTWBTV PA JOHNSTOWN
WGAL   PA LANCASTER
WLYHTV PA LANCASTER
KYWTV PA PHILADELPHIA ,
WPVITV PA PHILADELPHIA,
WCAU   PA PHILADELPHIA ,
WPHLTV PA PHILADELPHIA
WTXF   PA PHILADELPHIA
WYBE   PA PHILADELPHIA
WPSG   PA PHILADELPHIA
KDKATV PA PITTSBURGH
WTAETV PA PITTSBURGH
WPXI   PA PITTSBURGH
WQED   PA PITTSBURGH
WQEX   PA PITTSBURGH
WPTTTV PA PITTSBURGH
WPGHTV PA PITTSBURGH
WTVE   PA READING
WGCBTV PA RED LION
WNEPTV PA SCRANTON
WYOU   PA SCRANTON
WOLFTV PA SCRANTON
WVIATV PA SCRANTON
WSWBTV PA SCRANTON
WBRETV PA WILKES-BARRE
WILF   PA WILLIAMSPORT
WPMT   PA YORK
WOSTTV RI BLOCK ISLAND
WJAR   RI PROVIDENCE
WPRITV RI PROVIDENCE
WSBETV RI PROVIDENCE
WNACTV RI PROVIDENCE
WEBATV SC ALLENDALE
WFBCTV SC ANDERSON
WJWJTV SC BEAUFORT
WCBDTV SC CHARLESTON

WCIV   SC CHARLESTON
WCSCTV SC CHARLESTON
WITV   SC CHARLESTON
WTATTV SC CHARLESTON
WMMP   SC CHARLESTON
WIS   SC COLUMBIA
WLTX   SC COLUMBIA
WOLOTV SC COLUMBIA
WRLKTV SC COLUMBIA
WACH   SC COLUMBIA
WHMC   SC CONWAY
WBTW   SC FLORENCE
WPDETV SC FLORENCE
WWMB   SC FLORENCE
WJPMTV SC FLORENCE
WYFF   SC GREENVILLE
WGGSTV SC GREENVILLE
WNTV   SC GREENVILLE
WNEH   SC GREENWOOD
WTGS   SC HARDEEVILLE
WFXB   SC MYRTLE BEACH
WNSCTV SC ROCK HILL
WFVT   SC ROCK HILL
WSPATV SC SPARTANBURG
WRETTV SC SPARTANBURG
WRJATV SC SUMTER
WQHB   SC SUMTER
KABYTV SD ABERDEEN
KDSDTV SD ABERDEEN
KESDTV SD BROOKINGS
KPSDTV SD EAGLE BUTTE
KDLOTV SD FLORENCE
KTTM   SD HURON
KIVVTV SD LEAD
KHSDTV SD LEAD
KQSDTV SD LOWRY
KZSDTV SD MARTIN
KDLT   SD MITCHELL
KPRYTV SD PIERRE
KTSDTV SD PIERRE
KOTATV SD RAPID CITY
KEVNTV SD RAPID CITY
KBHETV SD RAPID CITY
KCLOTV SD RAPID CITY
KPLOTV SD RELIANCE
KELOTV SD SIOUX FALLS
KSFYTV SD SIOUX FALLS
KTTW   SD SIOUX FALLS
KCSDTV SD SIOUX FALLS
NEW   SD SIOUX FALLS

NEW   SD SIOUX FALLS
KUSDTV SD VERMILLION
WRCBTV TN CHATTANOOGA
WTVC   TN CHATTANOOGA
WDEFTV TN CHATTANOOGA
WTCI   TN CHATTANOOGA
WDSITV TN CHATTANOOGA
WFLI   TN CLEVELAND
WCTE   TN COOKEVILLE
WKZX   TN COOKEVILLE
WINT   TN CROSSVILLE
WEMT   TN GREENEVILLE
WPGD   TN HENDERSONVILLE
WBBJTV TN JACKSON
WMTU   TN JACKSON
WPMC   TN JELLICO
WJHLTV TN JOHNSON CITY
WKPTTV TN KINGSPORT
WATETV TN KNOXVILLE
WVLTTV TN KNOXVILLE
WBIRTV TN KNOXVILLE
WKOPTV TN KNOXVILLE
WTNZ   TN KNOXVILLE
WJFB   TN LEBANON
WLJTTV TN LEXINGTON
WREGTV TN MEMPHIS
WMCTV TN MEMPHIS
WKNO   TN MEMPHIS
WHBQTV TN MEMPHIS
WPTYTV TN MEMPHIS
WLMT   TN MEMPHIS
WFBI   TN MEMPHIS
WHTN   TN MURFREESBORO
WKRNTV TN NASHVILLE
WSMVTV TN NASHVILLE
WTVF   TN NASHVILLE
WDCN   TN NASHVILLE
WZTV   TN NASHVILLE
WUXP   TN NASHVILLE
WNAB   TN NASHVILLE
WSJKTV TN SNEEDVILLE
KRBCTV TX ABILENE
KTABTV TX ABILENE
KHSHTV TX ALVIN
KACVTV TX AMARILLO
KAMRTV TX AMARILLO
KVIITV TX AMARILLO
KFDATV TX AMARILLO
KCIT   TX AMARILLO

KINZ   TX ARLINGTON
KTBCTV TX AUSTIN
KLRU   TX AUSTIN
KVUETV TX AUSTIN
KXANTV TX AUSTIN
KEYETV TX AUSTIN
KNVA   TX AUSTIN
KVVV   TX BAYTOWN
KFDMTV TX BEAUMONT
KBMT   TX BEAUMONT
KITU   TX BEAUMONT
KNCT   TX BELTON
KWAB   TX BIG SPRING
KVEO   TX BROWNSVILLE
KBTXTV TX BRYAN
KYLE   TX BRYAN
KAMUTV TX COLLEGE STATION
KTFH   TX CONROE
KHIM   TX CONROE
KIII   TX CORPUS CHRISTI
KRISTV TX CORPUS CHRISTI
KZTV   TX CORPUS CHRISTI
KEDTTV TX CORPUS CHRISTI
KORO   TX CORPUS CHRISTI
KDFWTV TX DALLAS
WFAATV TX DALLAS
KERATV TX DALLAS
KDFITV TX DALLAS
KDAF   TX DALLAS
KXTXTV TX DALLAS
KDTXTV TX DALLAS
KMPX   TX DECATUR
KTRG   TX DEL RIO
KDTN   TX DENTON
KVAW   TX EAGLE PASS
KDBCTV TX EL PASO
KVIATV TX EL PASO
KTSMTV TX EL PASO
KCOS   TX EL PASO
KFOXTV TX EL PASO
KINTTV TX EL PASO
KSCE   TX EL PASO
KJLFTV TX EL PASO
KXASTV TX FORT WORTH
KTVT   TX FORT WORTH
KTXA   TX FORT WORTH
KFWD   TX FORT WORTH
KLTJ   TX GALVESTON
KTMD   TX GALVESTON

KUVN   TX GARLAND
KTAQ   TX GREENVILLE
KGBTTV TX HARLINGEN
KLUJ   TX HARLINGEN
KMBH   TX HARLINGEN
KPRCTV TX HOUSTON
KUHT   TX HOUSTON
KHOUTV TX HOUSTON
KTRKTV TX HOUSTON
KETH   TX HOUSTON
KTXH   TX HOUSTON
KRIV   TX HOUSTON
KHTV   TX HOUSTON
KZJL   TX HOUSTON
KHSXTV TX IRVING
KETKTV TX JACKSONVILLE
KNWSTV TX KATY
KRRT   TX KERRVILLE
KAKW   TX KILLEEN
KLDT   TX LAKE DALLAS
KGNSTV TX LAREDO
KVTV   TX LAREDO
KLDOTV TX LAREDO
KXAMTV TX LLANO
KFXK   TX LONGVIEW
KTXTTV TX LUBBOCK
KCBDTV TX LUBBOCK
KLBKTV TX LUBBOCK
KPTB   TX LUBBOCK
KAMC   TX LUBBOCK
KJTV   TX LUBBOCK
KTRE   TX LUFKIN
KNVO   TX MCALLEN
KMID   TX MIDLAND
KLSBTV TX NACOGDOCHES
KOSATV TX ODESSA
KWESTV TX ODESSA
KPEJ   TX ODESSA
KOCVTV TX ODESSA
KMLM   TX ODESSA
KJACTV TX PORT ARTHUR
KAIO   TX RIO GRANDE CITY
KXLNTV TX ROSENBERG
KACBTV TX SAN ANGELO
KIDY   TX SAN ANGELO
KLST   TX SAN ANGELO
KMOLTV TX SAN ANTONIO
KENSTV TX SAN ANTONIO
KLRN   TX SAN ANTONIO

KSATTV TX SAN ANTONIO
KHCE   TX SAN ANTONIO
KABB   TX SAN ANTONIO
KWEXTV TX SAN ANTONIO
KVDA   TX SAN ANTONIO
KXII   TX SHERMAN
KPCB   TX SNYDER
KTXSTV TX SWEETWATER
KCENTV TX TEMPLE
KTALTV TX TEXARKANA
KLTV   TX TYLER
KVCT   TX VICTORIA
KAVUTV TX VICTORIA
KWTXTV TX WACO
KXXV   TX WACO
KCTF   TX WACO
KWKT   TX WACO
KRGVTV TX WESLACO
KFDXTV TX WICHITA FALLS
KAUZTV TX WICHITA FALLS
KJTL   TX WICHITA FALLS
KSGITV UT CEDAR CITY
KULC   UT OGDEN
KOOGTV UT OGDEN
KBYUTV UT PROVO
KZARTV UT PROVO
KUTV   UT SALT LAKE CITY
KTVX   UT SALT LAKE CITY
KSLTV   UT SALT LAKE CITY
KUED   UT SALT LAKE CITY
KSTU   UT SALT LAKE CITY
KJZZTV UT SALT LAKE CITY
KUSG   UT ST. GEORGE
WTMW   VA ARLINGTON
WAWB   VA ASHLAND
WCYBTV VA BRISTOL
WVIRTV VA CHARLOTTESVILLE
WHTJ   VA CHARLOTTESVILLE
WDRLTV VA DANVILLE
WNVC   VA FAIRFAX
WVPY   VA FRONT ROYAL
WNVT   VA GOLDVEIN
WLFG   VA GRUNDY
WVECTV VA HAMPTON
WHROTV VA HAMPTON-NORFOLK
WHSVTV VA HARRISONBURG
WSETTV VA LYNCHBURG
WJPR   VA LYNCHBURG
WVVI   VA MANASSAS

WMSYTV VA MARION
WTKR   VA NORFOLK
WTVZ   VA NORFOLK
WJCB   VA NORFOLK
WSBNTV VA NORTON
WRICTV VA PETERSBURG
WAVYTV VA PORTSMOUTH
WGNT   VA PORTSMOUTH
WTVRTV VA RICHMOND
WWBT   VA RICHMOND
WCVETV VA RICHMOND
WRLHTV VA RICHMOND
WCVW   VA RICHMOND
WDBJ   VA ROANOKE
WSLSTV VA ROANOKE
WBRATV VA ROANOKE
WFXRTV VA ROANOKE
WEFC   VA ROANOKE
WVPT   VA STAUNTON
WVBT   VA VIRGINIA BEACH
WCAXTV VT BURLINGTON
WVNY   VT BURLINGTON
WETK   VT BURLINGTON
WFFFTV VT BURLINGTON
WNNETV VT HARTFORD
WVER   VT RUTLAND
WVTB   VT ST. JOHNSBURY
WVTA   VT WINDSOR
KBGE   WA BELLEVUE
KBEH   WA BELLEVUE
KVOSTV WA BELLINGHAM
KBCB   WA BELLINGHAM
KCKA   WA CENTRALIA
KONGTV WA EVERETT
KVEW   WA KENNEWICK
KEPRTV WA PASCO
KWSUTV WA PULLMAN
KNDU   WA RICHLAND
KTNW   WA RICHLAND
KOMOTV WA SEATTLE
KINGTV WA SEATTLE
KIROTV WA SEATTLE
KCTSTV WA SEATTLE
KTZZTV WA SEATTLE
KHCV   WA SEATTLE
KREMTV WA SPOKANE
KXLYTV WA SPOKANE
KHQTV   WA SPOKANE
KSPSTV WA SPOKANE
KSKN   WA SPOKANE

KAYUTV WA SPOKANE
KSTW WA TACOMA
KCPQ WA TACOMA
KTBWTV WA TACOMA
KBTCTV WA TACOMA
KWDK WA TACOMA
KPDX WA VANCOUVER
KCWT WA WENATCHEE
KNDO WA YAKIMA
KIMATV WA YAKIMA
KAPP WA YAKIMA
KYVE WA YAKIMA
WACY WI APPLETON
WEUX WI CHIPPEWA FALLS
WYOW WI EAGLE RIVER
WEAUTV WI EAU CLAIRE
WQOWTV WI EAU CLAIRE
WMMFTV WI FOND DU LAC
WBAYTV WI GREEN BAY
WFRVTV WI GREEN BAY
WLUKTV WI GREEN BAY
WGBA WI GREEN BAY
WPNE WI GREEN BAY
WJNW WI JANESVILLE
WHKE WI KENOSHA
WKBT WI LA CROSSE
WXOWTV WI LA CROSSE
WLAX WI LA CROSSE
WHLATV WI LA CROSSE
WISCTV WI MADISON
WMTV WI MADISON
WHATV WI MADISON
WKOWTV WI MADISON
WMSNTV WI MADISON
WTHXTV WI MANITOWOC
WWRS WI MAYVILLE
WHWCTV WI MENOMONIE
WTMJTV WI MILWAUKEE
WITITV WI MILWAUKEE
WMVS WI MILWAUKEE
WISNTV WI MILWAUKEE
WVTV WI MILWAUKEE
WCGVTV WI MILWAUKEE
WVCYTV WI MILWAUKEE
WMVT WI MILWAUKEE
WDJTTV WI MILWAUKEE
WLEFTV WI PARK FALLS
WJJA WI RACINE
WJFWTV WI RHINELANDER

KBJRTV WI SUPERIOR
WSCO WI SURING
WSAWTV WI WAUSAU
WAOWTV WI WAUSAU
WHRMTV WI WAUSAU
WVVA WV BLUEFIELD
WLFB WV BLUEFIELD
WCHSTV WV CHARLESTON
WVAHTV WV CHARLESTON
WKRPTV WV CHARLESTON
WBOYTV WV CLARKSBURG
WLYJ WV CLARKSBURG
WSWPTV WV GRANDVIEW
WSAZTV WV HUNTINGTON
WOWKTV WV HUNTINGTON
WPBYTV WV HUNTINGTON
WVSX WV LEWISBURG
WSHE WV MARTINSBURG
WNPBTV WV MORGANTOWN
WOAYTV WV OAK HILL
WTAPTV WV PARKERSBURG
WDTV WV WESTON
WTRFTV WV WHEELING
KTWOTV WY CASPER
KGWCTV WY CASPER
KFNB WY CASPER
KGWNTV WY CHEYENNE
KLWY WY CHEYENNE
KKTU WY CHEYENNE
KJWY WY JACKSON
KCWCTV WY LANDER
KGWLTV WY LANDER
KFNR WY RAWLINS
KFNE WY RIVERTON
KGWRTV WY ROCK SPRINGS
KSGWTV WY SHERIDAN

Supporters Index

Index For Geographic Location

Alaska

Anchorage Daily News
Anchorage, AK

Arizona

Environmental Fund for Arizona
Phoenix or Tucson, AZ

Arkansas

The Arkansas Educational
Telecommunications Network
Conway, AR

California

1492 Pictures
Los Angeles, CA

Academy of Television Arts & Sciences
North Hollywood, CA

AIDS Walk San Francisco
San Francisco, CA

The Bakersfield Californian
Bakersfield, CA

Chevron Corporation
San Francisco, CA

CinePartners Entertainment
Los Angeles, CA

CNET, Inc. The Computer Network
San Francisco, CA

Digital Domain
Venice, CA

Digital Imagination
Westlake Village, CA

DreamWorks
Universal City, CA

EHQ, Inc.
Hollywood, CA

Experience America
San Francisco, CA

Forests Forever
San Francisco, CA

Free Arts for Abused Children
Los Angeles, CA

H-Gun West
San Francisco, CA

The Jim Henson Company
Hollywood, CA

Industrial Light & Magic
San Rafael, CA

International Cartoons & Animation
Center, Inc.
Santa Ana, CA

Intrepidus Worldwide
Santa Monica, CA

Jews for Jesus
San Francisco, CA

KGTV, San Diego's 10
San Diego, CA

KQED TV
San Francisco, CA

KRON-TV Channel 7
San Francisco, CA

KTLA-TV
Los Angeles, CA
Landor Associates
San Francisco, CA

LAUNCH Media
Santa Monica, CA
Lucasfilm Ltd. and Lucas Licensing Ltd.
San Rafael, CA

M80 Interactive Marketing
Los Angeles, CA

Minorities in Broadcasting Training
Program
Los Angeles, CA

The Nautilus Institute for Security and
Sustainable Development
Berkeley, CA

Nickelodeon Animation Studio
Burbank, CA

Paradesa Media
San Francisco, CA

The Partos Company
Los Angeles, CA

The Presidio Trust
San Francisco, CA

Pixar Animation Studios
Richmond, CA

Rhyhm and Hues
Los Angeles, CA

Sendmail, Inc.
Emeryville, CA

Skywalker Sound
San Rafael, CA

SOL Design FX
Santa Monica, CA

Southern Exposure
San Francisco, CA

StandUp For Kids
Chula Vista, CA

Walt Disney Feature Animation
Burbank, CA

World Children's Transplant Fund
Encino, CA
Xerox Research & Technology
Palo Alto, CA

Colorado

KWGN-TV WB2
Englewood, CO

Connecticut

Wadsworth Atheneum
Hartford, CT

Florida

CFN-13
Orlando, FL

Compulab Inc.
Miami, FL

M&M Creative Services
Tallahassee, FL

Marco Island Film Festival
Marco Island, FL

Universal City Florida
Orlando, FL

Walt Disney Feature Animation
Lake Buena Vista, FL

WFOR-TV CBS 4 News
Miami, FL

Georgia

CNN TalkBack Live
Atlanta, GA

Cox Interactive Media
Atlanta, GA

McKessonHBOC
Alpharetta, GA

Tribune Broadcasting
Atlanta, GA

Illinois

Chicago Peace Museum
Chicago, IL

CLTV News, Chicago
Oak Brook, IL

GenneX Healthcare Technologies
Chicago, IL

H-Gun Labs
Chicago, IL

Moline Dispatch Publishing Company
Rock Island, IL

Morningstar, Inc.
Chicago, IL

Museum of Contemporary Art
Chicago, IL

SWIFTT, Inc.
Rockford, IL

Tribune Media Services
Chicago, IL

WBBM TV (CBS)
Chicago, IL

Indiana

TUV Productions rrr by ABC of Film
Indianapolis, IN

WNDU-TV
South Bend, IN

WXIN-TV
Indianapolis, IN

Kentucky

EarthSave International
Louisville, KY

Massachusetts

American Training of Massachusetts
Lawrence, MA

Arts & Education Corporation
Marblehead, MA

Ingalls
Boston, MA

Life Online Network, Inc.
Boston, MA

Media Education Foundation
Northampton, MA

MonsterSwapper.com
Westborough, MA

NOVA Online
Boston, MA

Schwartz & Associates
Boston, MA

Smarter Living, Inc.
Cambridge, MA

Universal Studios
Burlington, MA

WB56
Boston, MA

WWLP TV22
Springfield, MA

The Weber Group
Burlington, MA

Maryland

Baltimore Magazine
Baltimore, MD

WMAR TV (ABC)
Baltimore, MD

Michigan

The Freep
Detroit, MI

Issle Royale National Park
Houghton, MI

Minnesota

Harvest Moon Community Farm
Scandia, MN

MJM Family Cancer Services
St. Paul, MN

Missouri

LiveWire Marketing, Inc.
Chesterfield, MO

Montana

KPAX TV (CBS)
Missoula, MT

North Carolina

The North Carolina State Parks System
Raleigh, NC

North Dakota

Community Access Television
Bismarck, ND

New Jersey

The Dow Jones Newspaper Fund
Princeton, NJ

New York

Amp NYC Animation
New York, NY

Animate NYC
New York, NY

Aperture Foundation
New York, NY

Archive Films/Archive Photos
New York, NY

Artbear Pigmation, Inc.
Ithaca, NY

Association for Independent Video &
Filmmakers
New York, NY

BNN
New York, NY

Buzzco Associates, Inc.
New York, NY

CBS News
New York, NY

Center for Photography at Woodstock
Woodstock, NY

Children's Television Workshop
New York, NY

Creative Time
New York, NY

CultureFinder.com
New York, NY

Curious Pictures
New York, NY

David Findlay Jr. Fine Art
New York, NY

Easynett.com, Inc.
New York, NY
Film/Video Arts
New York, NY

The Jim Henson Company
New York, NY

Historic Films
East Hampton, NY

Jinil Au Chocolat
Cedarhurst, NY

KBEG Inc.
New York, NY

Lovett Productions, Inc.
New York, NY

Marvel Entertainment Group, Inc.
New York, NY

MTV, Music Television
New York, NY

NARAL of New York
New York, NY

New York Times
New York, NY

R/GA Digital Studio
New York, NY

REI Media Group
New York, NY

Richmond Communications LLC
New York, NY

Soap Opera Digest
New York, NY

Sunbow Entertainment
New York, NY

WNBC
New York, NY

Women Make Movies, Inc.
New York, NY

WTVH-5
Syracuse, NY

Zooma Zooma
New York, NY

Ohio

WTOV-TV9
Steubenville, OH

Oregon

Columbia Pacific Community Information
Center
Astoria, OR

Portland Art Museum, Northwest Film
Center
Portland, OR

Pennsylvania

WHP-TV/UPN 15 WLYH
Harrisburg, PA

WNEP-TV 16
Moosic, PA

WPMT-TV Fox 43
York, PA

WTXF-FOX
Philadelphia, PA

Texas

Hodges and Associates
Dallas, TX

WFAA TV (ABC)
Dallas, TX

KVUE TV (ABC)
Austin, TX

Virgina

American Association of School
Administrators
Arlington, VA

Central Intelligence Agency
Arlington, VA

Frank Beach and Associates, Inc.
Arlington, VA

Universal Systems Inc. (USI)
Chantilly, VA

Virginia Museum of Fine Arts
Richmond, VA

WDBJ 7
Roanoke, VA

Washington

KCPQ
Seattle, WA

Washington, DC

Center on Policy Attitudes
of Washington, DC
Washington, DC

Families USA Foundation
Washington, DC

Robert M. Brandon & Associates
Washington, DC

The Naval Historical Center
Washington, DC

The Office of Imaging, Printing and
Photographic Services
Washington, DC

Wave Works Digital Media
Washington, DC

Wisconsin

College Grad Job Hunter, Inc.
Cedarburg, WI

General Index

1492 Pictures 48

A

Academy of Television Arts & Sciences 48
AIDS Walk San Francisco 50
American Association of School
    Administrators 51
American Training of Massachusetts 52
Amp NYC Animation 53
Anchorage Daily News 53
Animate NYC 54
Aperture Foundation 55
Archive Films/Archive Photos 56
Arkansas Educational Telecommunications
    Network 56
Artbear Pigmation, Inc. 58
Arts & Education Corporation 59

B

Bakersfield Californian 62
Baltimore Magazine 61
Beach and Associates, Inc. 99
BNN 63
Brandon & Associates, Robert M. 168
ByLandSeaAndAir.Com 65

C

CBS News 65
Center for Photography at Woodstock 66
Center on Policy Attitudes of Washington,
    DC 67
Central Intelligence Agency 68